from *Jenin* to **Gaza**

a short visit to a long conflict

From Jenin to Gaza:

A short visit to a long conflict

Silvio Cerulli

First published 2003
by
Beyond the Pale
BTP Publications Ltd
Unit 2.1.2 Conway Mill
5-7 Conway Street
Belfast BT13 2DE

Tel: +44 (0)28 90 438630
Fax: +44 (0)28 90 439707
E-mail: office@btpale.com
Website: http://www.btpale.com

British Library Cataloguing-in-Publication Data.
A catalogue record for this book is available from the British Library.

ISBN 1-900960-22-2
Printed in Dublin by Colour Books Ltd.

To Sofia

May she walk one day the beaches of Gaza
and sing along with the children from Jenin.

*This book is part of a wider charity project
destined to help the children from the primary school in
the Aida refugee camp, just outside Bethlehem.
The proceeds from the book will be given to the school
and its children.*

Beach Camp,
Gaza City

Contents

Acknowledgments

Throughout these pages I am not trying to present an in-depth, historical and political analysis of the conflict in the Middle East. While reaffirming the Palestinians' rights, I am not negating the needs of the Israelis. Still the story takes place in the Occupied Territories, where injustice is blatant.

This is just a short journey, primarily through our consciences rather than through Palestine. These are simply facts, monologues of pre-announced deaths. It is only a moment in an ancient dispute, but worth telling for those children.

It is hard to find the correct words to thank the following people for their support, wisdom and patience: Father Des Wilson, Helen Pope and Roberto Capocelli, Antonietta Ricciardi-McCarthy and Rudie Goldsmith, Agnieszka and Mike, Bill, Mustapha, Salah, Samid, Ivan Bonfanti, Giancarlo Lannutti, Kay McCarthy, Peadar Whelan, Ali Halimeh, Claudia, Yousef, Nadir, Mary and Lucia.

A profound thanks to the men, women, children and elderly people of Jenin and Gaza for the love they taught me in such difficult circumstances.

Finally, it is hard to explain in words the depth of gratitude I owe my partner and, last but not least, my son Luca for protecting me from the 'bad boys'. This work could not have been completed without them.

Preface

Palestinians are grateful to Silvio for this important contribution to truth and justice. Silvio's attempt to highlight the plight of the Palestinian people is another testimony to the international dimension of the conflict.

We have long called for international intervention, yet while governments have looked on impotently, hesitated to speak out and failed to prevent the acts of terror perpetrated by the state of Israel, it is the international community of people and human beings who have been the true 'united nations' peace keepers.

It is in individuals like Silvio who have bravely observed and told the truth about violations of human rights and international law, and volunteers like Mary Kelly and Caoimhe Butterly who have helped to get medical supplies through to people trapped or under siege, brought food to those who are starving and clean water to people whose supplies have been cut off or contaminated.

This book bears witness to the tragedy of the terrible human and material destruction caused by the recent Israeli military invasions into Palestinian towns, villages and refugee camps. But very importantly, it also tells the story of the daily oppression of the Palestinian people who have suffered for too long under the illegal Israeli occupation.

I hope this book helps you, the reader, to gain a deeper understanding of the everyday realities faced by the Palestinian people, which while devastating and cruel, are often left out of the news. I hope that it also gives you a clearer insight into the history and context of the conflict and therefore the reasons for our struggle to achieve full independence, to realise our human rights and to see the prospect of peace one day become a reality.

Silvio's commitment and that of other soldiers of peace to the just cause of Palestine gives us the hope and optimism to continue this struggle to achieve our freedom. Israel and those who support its aggression against the Palestinian people cannot shake our determination to achieve it. Silvio's message strengthens our resolve to defeat the occupation of our land – Palestine shall be free.

Ambassador Ali Halimeh
Ireland

1.

The road to Jenin

The Apache helicopter shakes the foggy clouds over the thick olive groves around Salem, north of Jenin, which lies at the very bottom of my heart and on the border between desperation and dismay.

A primary school, a shop, a mosque and a few derelict houses built around a ridge make the village of Salem one of the most northern outposts of the Palestinian territories on the West Bank.

Children raise their hands in a high five and wave victory signs; women dressed in black walk out of the empty market. Salem is situated on the slopes of the Samarian Hills and only a few miles from the Golan Heights and the Israeli-Lebanese border. At the bottom of the village, in an area transformed into a military camp, a detention centre erected for those arrested in Jenin lies exactly where the Green Line once passed. Among the Merkava 3, the huge Israeli tanks, soldiers are cleaning two freezer-containers, we are told, used to transport dead bodies.

On the top of the ridge there is an unpaved parking lot, partially occupied by a huge pile of black plastic bags. They are full of clothes from the surrounding villages and they will be brought to the people of the refugee camp as soon as the military curfew is lifted. The attack on Jenin began on April 2, 2002, and since then the town has been declared a no-go area for international observers and media.

A few days ago, however, members of Amnesty International and some journalists have found a gap in the Israeli iron ring and have succeeded in reaching the refugee camp on the outskirts of Jenin. There could be hundreds of dead bodies there. Nearly two weeks into Operation Defensive Shield, launched by Sharon after the death of 38 Israeli civilians in two separate suicide attacks in the nearby towns of Netanya and Haifa, the military repression seems far from over.

I enter through that same gap hours after the pioneers. The journey into the death camp starts from the top of Salem ridge. A local guide leads two French reporters and myself down the steep hill covered with wild bushes. Another helicopter has replaced the Apache above the morning fog; clouds are entangled on the rolling hills.

Half way down the slope there is a red-dirt road; an army jeep patrols it every ten/fifteen minutes. We duck down between the rocks waiting for the army and once the jeep has disappeared, we undertake a two-hour long walk on tortuous footpaths, under cover of centuries-old olive trees. Like a diving vulture the helicopter obliges us to stop countless times. Journalists, medics, monks, pacifists, UN and Red Cross personnel, international observers have all been killed without regard by the IDF (Israel Defence Force), as the Israelis familiarly call their army.

Dogs barking in the distance make us hasten our steps; adrenaline fights the scorching heat under the heavy bullet-proof jacket. The tiny village of Rumaneh, our destination, is so near that we can hear the locals chatting when we spot an Israeli foot patrol walking parallel to us, some 80 yards to our right, across an empty field. We jump into a ditch while the Israeli soldiers stop at the roadside and call by radio; it will be ten minutes before an army personnel carrier picks them up. It will take much more time before our hearts resume their normal rhythm.

During the attack ordinary Palestinians and foreign journalists outside the city have seen hundreds of missiles being fired into the camp. The sight of such firepower being aimed at Jenin leads those who witnessed the raids, including military experts and the media, to believe that scores of civilians have been killed. The tight security cordon means that the outside world has no means of knowing what is happening in the camp and those who breached the iron ring at risk to their own lives have only seen a

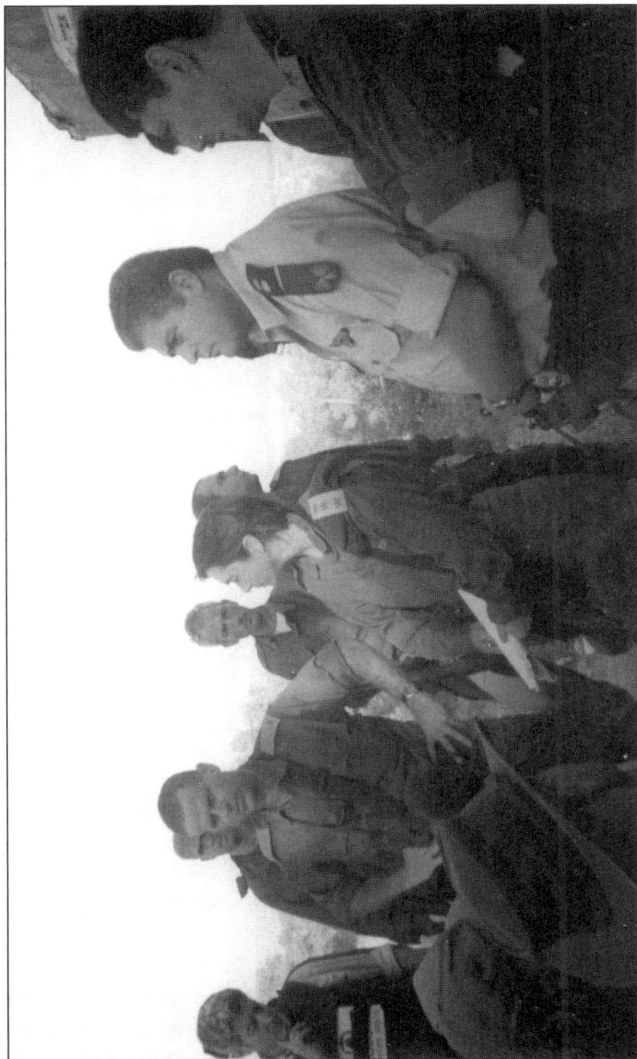

Brigadier General Shlein (the officer on the far left), during a military briefing between Salem and Jenin. He was divisional commander for all military operations in the Jenin area.

small portion of the camp. It is in these circumstances that reports of a massacre are quickly spreading.

Stories from the refugee camp are only starting to unfold, but the local people are claiming that a carnage has been perpetrated and numerous indications lead in that direction. The first reports from Jenin, coupled with Shimon Peres[1] comment that he fears 'a massacre was committed' and the words of an army officer in Jenin – 'the damage that will be done to Israel once the world sees the inside of the camp, it's too hard to contemplate' – appear to confirm the accusations. If Shimon Peres went as far as mentioning the taboo word 'massacre', it is a sign that something dreadful must have happened. Army spokespersons have first spoken of 200 Palestinians killed; after Peres' words, only hours later, the death toll has already been cut by half.

But how can Jenin be reached? Where does it all start?

For the Jews, after 20 centuries of being persecuted and dispersed, this land is the home of their ancestors, who had invaded Palestine before the birth of time. On the other hand the Arabs have never had sovereignty over the area because of continued occupations, but they had nevertheless lived in Palestine since before the dawn of history. Palestine remained an Arab country up to the end of the World War One when it was the British who imposed the Jewish community on the Arabs.[2]

In a way, it started in the concentration camps towards the end of World War Two. In the aftermath of the Nazi Holocaust, in which six million Jews were exterminated, the newly-created United Nations proposed the partition of Palestine into three territories: an Arab state, a Jewish one and international status for Jerusalem. The foundation of the Israeli state was warmly welcomed all around although the Arabs were implacably hostile to it. In giving the Jews a land they were linked to by the holy scriptures but divided by two thousand years, the UN was taking it away from the indigenous people.

By allocating 77.94 percent of Palestine to the Jews, the UN was actually planting the seeds of racial hatred which still bears the poisoned fruit of the present strife. The Gaza Strip fell under

Egyptian control while the West Bank, established in 1948, came under Jordanian jurisdiction.

More than 750,000 Palestinians, or three quarters of the native population, were forced to leave their home country because of the war – state-terrorism for the Arabs – and become refugees in neighbouring states. Thirteen thousand were killed. Once completely depopulated, 418 cities, towns and villages were razed to the ground.[3] Rejected by many bordering countries, thousands of refugees finally found shelter when the UN opened camps in Jordan, Lebanon, Syria and Gaza. In other words, the Jewish refugee problem was apparently solved by creating a Palestinian refugee problem.

A few hours after the Israeli declaration of independence, on May 14, 1948, the Arab League promised 'a massacre': Syrian soldiers occupied Upper Galilee while the Iraqis stopped just ten miles from the Mediterranean Sea and the Egyptian Army reached the outskirts of Tel Aviv. On May 25 the League broke into Jerusalem's Old City but their military supremacy was not to last. Gradually the Israelis regained the land previously lost during the first weeks of war (with the exception of the Old City) and moved further, conquering new territories in Galilee and in the Negev Desert; only the Gaza Strip, bordering on the Sinai region, remained in Arab hands. The armistice was declared in July 1949 but the political geography of the Middle East had been reshaped for good.

During the 1950s, Egypt became the focus for anti-Israeli feelings, especially after General Nasser emerged as the leader of Arab nationalism. In 1956 Israel invaded the Sinai Desert, supported by British and French troops, and in just 100 hours reached the Suez Canal. The occupation lasted six months and after they withdrew, the Gaza Strip was placed under United Nations control. Less than ten years later, allied with Syria and Jordan, the Egyptians staged a bloody comeback but with a series of armed actions regarded as one of the quickest and most overwhelming engagements in military history, the Israelis destroyed their enemy's air and land forces in just six days. It became known as the Six Day War (1967), produced 340,000 new Palestinian refugees and expanded Israeli territories after the conquest of Gaza, the Golan Heights, Jerusalem and the whole of Palestine to the west bank of the River Jordan.

These areas were not returned; quite the contrary, they were placed under military administration. In the West Bank around 150,000 people were forced to flee. The occupation was met by public sector strikes, student mobilisation[4] and guerrilla activity. Tel Aviv responded with increased military repression and the building of settlements began almost immediately. In 1973 Egypt and Israel began peace negotiations; eventually Israeli Prime Minister Begin and Egyptian President Sadat were rewarded the Nobel Peace Prize for their 1979 peace agreement.

However, the Israeli-Egyptian deal was strongly rejected by Palestinian nationalists; since the 1960s their mainstream group, the Palestine Liberation Organization (PLO), had gradually intensified its campaign on Israeli targets mainly from its Jordanian and Lebanese bases. On June 6, 1982, the Israeli army crossed its northern frontier, invaded Lebanon and for years to follow bombed the refugee camps while the Fedayeen (Arab partisans) retaliated against Israel. Beirut became synonymous with bombings and massacres, before the Israelis pulled out in 1985. A Jew who was only a boy on his arrival to the promised land in 1948 may have already fought five conflicts in less than four decades, without mentioning the two Palestinian Intifadas.

The first insurrection – a direct expression of the Palestinian right to resist and had nothing to do with terrorism and violence – erupted in 1987 and lasted six years (with 640 Palestinians and about 40 Israelis killed). It ended with the Declaration of Principles, an historical but controversial turning point. This was regarded as the biggest breakthrough in the Palestinian question and it was in itself the first-ever peace deal between Israel and an Arab authority.

The peace agreement negotiated in Oslo and Washington in 1993 defined the territories along the so-called Green Line, recognizing the Palestinian state within the West Bank and the Gaza Strip in the form of the Palestinian National Authority (PNA). The whole of these territories, including East Jerusalem, corresponds to just 22 percent of the entire land of Palestine before Israel came into being.[5]

As a result of the agreement, the Palestinians were required to offer peace ('security' according to the Israelis), which is mainly a state of mental being. The state of Israel was supposed to promptly return land which is something concrete. But for many Palestinians, and not only them, the Oslo Agreement was 'a capitulation by means of which Israel achieved all its political and strategic objectives, gaining recognition and legitimacy without, in effect, conceding anything apart from a bland acceptance of the PLO as the representative of the Palestinian people, giving them an authority they could in no way exercise.'[6]

This is the main reason why, since 1993, different Israeli prime ministers have struggled to sabotage and delay the implementation of the Oslo agreements; one of them, Yitzak Rabin, who had concluded the peace talks, was killed by one of his own people in Tel Aviv.

In February 2001, pledging to deliver 'peace and security', Ariel Sharon's right wing Likud Party won the election and the former army general became premier. According to many observers, although the peace process was already in tatters, it was the controversial visit by Sharon to the al-Aqsa Mosque in Jerusalem five months earlier, during which five Palestinians were killed by police and army, that sparked the present uprising. That is why many Arabs refer to it as the 'al-Aqsa Intifada'.

Sharon's complete disregard for human rights and international law soon drove Palestinian militants into taking even more desperate and unjustifiable actions. Reoccupation of the territories, military repression, mass murder of civilians and economic apartheid forced some Palestinians to turn themselves into human weapons: the 'shaheed' (Arabic for 'martyr').

It may be argued that such a tragic and counter-productive form of resistance had rarely been adopted in similar circumstances throughout the world, yet the diabolical nature of the Israeli persecution of the Palestinians remains incomparable.

Probably the only way to stop the martyrs is to offer them a glimpse of hope. They know that what the Palestinians had lost in 1948 is forever gone; so, can 'terrorism' still be an option in a dream to restore what is humanly and physically irreversible? Last year only, 20 suicide bombers brought death and grief into the heart of Israel, by targeting Haifa, Tel Aviv, Jerusalem. Dozens of people, the vast majority civilians, have lost their lives as a result of these attacks.

By the beginning of 2002, nine years after Oslo, over three million Palestinians were caged in about 230 autonomous pockets which intermittently come under curfew and incursions by the Israeli army. In many cases they are literally imprisoned in their own district, in their own town, virtually cut off from the rest of the country. By now dreams of peace, like cut flowers, are slowly withering and perishing.

On a warm February evening in Bethlehem, during a lunch with some friends, I remember being 'warned' about a new type of 10-kilometre range missile, the 'Qassam Two', capable of pounding Israeli cities from within the Palestinian territories. Only a week later one was fired, probably only to be tested, landing on waste ground inside an Israeli settlement in the Gaza Strip. This will prove to be one more turning point and the progressive escalation of violence has yet to stop. The last stretch of the road to Jenin starts here.

Sharon immediately grabbed the opportunity presented by these so far primitive and inaccurate weapons hand-made by Hamas militants. Aware of the damage inflicted on the Israeli forces by the Katyushas unleashed by the Hizbullah on northern Israel, Sharon ordered the creation of a ten-kilometre exclusion zone along the Green Line, the Gaza Strip borders and around the settlements.

Obviously the old warmonger doesn't restrict his vengeance to a mere exclusion zone; the missile attacks will be met with a very fierce Israeli response. Those who will lose their lives will be children, refugees, ordinary Palestinians, Israeli settlers, Israeli soldiers and civilians, all victims of the same absurdity. No one is excluded; Sharon's political blindness makes no distinctions.

Twenty one civilians and 22 PNA policemen were killed in the Gaza Strip in early February 2002, along with seven Israeli soldiers. For sheer retaliation, Gaza suffered nightly air-raids for 12 days in a row. For the first time since the beginning of the Intifada, Israeli tanks rolled into Gaza City centre while battleships kept shelling from the Mediterranean. The attack ended in the middle of March and was regarded as 'the most extensive army assault in the Gaza Strip in recent times'. In the West Bank 35 people were murdered when the IDF stormed the Jenin and Talaba refugee camps. Dozens of Palestinians died in Nablus, Ramallah, Beit Jala, Hebron.

Once again, like perfect mirrors, each side blamed the other one, while swapping atrocity for atrocity, but that is enough for the 'al-Aqsa Martyr Brigades', extremists formed by single members of the resistance movement. On Saturday March 2, the day for the Sabbath prayers, the first human bomb in two months killed nine Orthodox Jews leaving their Jerusalem synagogue. Two of the victims were children. A few hours later a lone sniper, using what was described as a World War Two carbine, fired 24 rounds in two minutes on a checkpoint in Ofra (West Bank), killing in quick sequence seven soldiers and three settlers before vanishing beyond the rocky hills.

Sharon convened his cabinet and in a speech to the nation spoke about 'the need to inflict heavier losses' on the Palestinians. In the short space of an hour two cars were blown up by tank shells in Ramallah. Inside it were a woman and five children on their last journey to school. A number of captured suicide bombers were executed while handcuffed, face downwards, shot in the head at close range. Fourteen people were murdered in Gaza, 73 refugees were slaughtered in a five-day IDF incursion in Tulkarm; on the sixth day the army pulled out of the camp, returning later, on International Women's Day, to obliterate 45 people in a very short time span.

Inevitably, such disproportionate military repression ended up feeding the never-ending cycle of attacks and reprisals. When two human bombs killed 22 civilians in Netanya and 16 in Haifa on Easter weekend, Sharon declared a 'war without borders on the Palestinians', ignored two new UN Resolutions issued in late March calling for Israeli withdrawal from the Territories, and invaded the West Bank with a fury unparalleled in his country's short history.

According to Israeli intelligence, the 'shaheed' responsible for the two latest bombings came from the Nablus-Jenin area. But was the assault on a civilian population justifiable by the presence of 'martyr cells'?

When we reach Rumaneh the locals welcome us with water and mint tea. A column of five tractors is parked in the dusty alleyway; the trailers have been hidden away because they might be spotted by the helicopters. Their cargo of flour, rice, milk, vegetables and fruit has been piled in the archipelago of small villages around Jenin. As soon as the sun settles tonight, they will risk their lives to bring relief to the besieged people trapped in the camp.

While we are waiting for a brave taxi driver who ships people into the closed military zone, a group of about 20 females arrives; elderly, women, girls, children, they are refugees who have fled the camp and they are shaken, exhausted, clearly still very frightened.

The first live accounts prepare us for the worst; something terrible must have happened. 'The soldiers grouped some of the men in the ruins of a house', a woman recalls; 'then they blew up the ruins and cleaned the scene with their bulldozers'.

'They blew open the doors with dynamite, entered the houses with their camouflaged black faces, placing mines in the rooms where families and children were hiding, to force them not to move', adds a girl in her twenties with a red stain of fresh blood on her bandaged hand. 'The camp smells of death due to the scattered bodies. Some bodies are buried under the rubble, others are crushed by tanks and the rest are left lying in the streets.'

Beside a lone, blossoming tree an old refugee thanks everyone for their help and support, but turning towards a Canadian observer she begs: 'It's not food that we really need. We will rebuild our homes and we can teach our children to starve; we can show them how to resist. What we really need is justice.'

Notes

1. Israel's Foreign Affairs Minister and leader of the Labour Party which joined the national unity government coalition.
2. With the Ottoman Empire fighting along with the Germans during World War One, Britain started to cultivate local Arab allies to defend its interests in the Suez Canal. Since 1917 the Zionist Movement became a key player and its power of persuasion resulted in the Balfour Declaration. On November 2, 1917, the then Foreign Secretary announced that 'His majesty's government viewed with favour the establishment of a national home in Palestine for the Jewish people'. British troops entered Palestine in 1918 and set up a provisional military government in Jerusalem. Britain had thus physically laid claim to a territory not only previously promised to both Arabs and Jews, but also designated as an internationally established zone. Anticipating the future dismemberment of the Ottoman Empire, Britain and France carved the Middle East into spheres of influence to prevent a power vacuum and Russia's entry into the region. British military presence from 1918 onwards assured Britain that it was granted the mandate over Palestine by the newly formed League of Nations; it gave London control over Palestine and Transjordan territories (they partitioned the latter into a separate kingdom, today's Jordan, in 1921). By the end of War World Two, Britain's policy for Palestine was in ruins. They tried to prevent Jews from heading for the Holy Land, adding to the horrors they had suffered in Europe. Jewish terrorists destroyed railways, bridges and raided military camps until July 22, 1946, when the British headquarters in Jerusalem was blown up by Irgun (a Jewish terrorist group). Ninety one people were killed. Two years later, in May 1948, the British finally withdrew.
3. According to Palestinian historians the actual figure stands at 531 towns and villages destroyed and replaced by 161 Israeli settlements by 1950. In the Deir Yassin village, just outside Jerusalem, 250 Palestinian men, women and children were slaughtered. In his book The Revolt, the future Israeli prime minister Menechem Begin admitted candidly and with the addition of blood-curdling details, that he had been responsible for the massacre.

4. Led by Bir Zeit University, a few miles north of Jerusalem.
5. The Deal required the Israeli government recognition of the PLO, withdrawal from Gaza and Jericho and additional unspecified withdrawals over an interim five-year period. In exchange, the PLO recognised Israel and promised to suppress 'terrorism'. Central issues like borders, sovereignty, refugees, water, Jerusalem and settlements were reserved for the so-called 'final status talks'. As the Israeli writer Amos Oz confessed in a BBC interview, 'the signing of the 1993 Agreement was the second biggest victory in the history of Zionism'. However on the ground, among the steep hills of the West Bank, the situation – if possible – is even worse than in 1993, when the Palestinian territories were still a unitary whole despite military occupation. After Oslo they were divided and sub-divided into separate reserves.
6. Edward W. Said, *Peace and its Discontents*. Vintage, 1995.

2.

The death camp

Before the start of the Defensive Shield operation there were about 14,000 people, more then half of them under the age of 18, living in the Jenin refugee camp. They were persecuted and exiled from their homes in the Haifa district in 1948; they were assaulted and decimated during the first Intifada (179 deaths), which promoted Jenin as the focal point of Palestinian resistance.

Jenin lies at the end of the Jezreel valley near the biblical site of Megiddo, better known as Armageddon, where the Book of Revelations prophesies that the final battle to end all earthly battles will one day be fought. The city is proud of its long militant history: 30 years (1918-1948) under British rule followed by 54 years of Israeli occupation made Jenin synonymous with insurrection and defiance. Izzedin Al Qassam, the Muslim preacher who led a bloody revolt in the region against British rule in the 1930s, is seen as a local hero. Born in Syria, and moving later to Haifa, he organized the resistance movement against the British and the Zionists from Jenin. Izzedin Al Qassam fell victim to a British Army ambush in northern Samaria on November 10, 1935. The military wing of Hamas named itself after him. In 1938 London acquired four tons of explosives to raze Jenin to the ground using human shields to cross the minefields. Thanks to the city's resistance, the British plot failed miserably.

In 1967, when a young Yasser Arafat returned clandestinely from his exile in Jordan to regroup the Palestinian resistance, he chose Jenin as his base. Furthermore after Jericho and Gaza, which were given back as the first step of the Agreement, Jenin was the first of all the other towns to be handed to the Palestinian Authority; this occurred on October 25, 1995. However, before the second insurrection began, Jenin was one of the Palestinian cities with the closest links to Israel. The town lies only 12 kilometres from the Green Line; many families living here have relatives in Israel and a large number of Palestinians worked there, while many Israelis came to Jenin to purchase cheap goods.

From Rumaneh the swaying taxi leaves the rocky path and takes a short cut through a field only partially protected by two lanes of trees, heading for the refugee camp. I look at the houses through the window and I wonder what it is like inside. Probably not even the IDF army chiefs have a total grasp of the overall picture and of the extent to which their soldiers have acted here.

After the driver has dropped us off beside a derelict hut once used for farming, we find ourselves at the edge of the camp. Lying on the slope of a hill the place is plunged into an unreal silence, brutally interrupted by the roar of the Merkavas thundering into the city. Dunes of debris mark the spot where a row of houses once stood.

We venture in as the silence gets thicker and deeper. The first human encounter – the military curfew is still in place – is a woman who points at the spot where she saw a dozen young people being 'murdered by Israeli troops; some were naked, others blind-folded', she relates; we find no bodies but the walls are riddled with gun-fire holes of all sizes.

We sneak into the town holding our breath, guided by hands signalling from windows and people whispering to indicate the short cuts to us. Three separate families offered us protection from the army patrol. A few yards into the camp the nauseating stink of the uncollected garbage which has been set alight floats in the motionless heat.

Although aware of the necessity of avoiding sudden noises which may attract unfriendly attention with so many IDF snipers on the roofs of buildings, almost suddenly I realize that I am walking on a jumble of broken glass, window frames and ceramic tiles, cracking at every step. Bits of mattresses, a marble, a denture and a pram are trapped in the rubble, fragments of ordinary life reduced to ash and crumbled debris.

Even though Palestinian armed resistance ceased a few days ago, Israeli snipers still open fire, usually to scare women and children. During a suspension in the curfew a young woman was walking toward the Jenin hospital to see the body of her son, killed during IDF shelling; as she was approaching the hospital she heard shooting and saw a five year old boy sitting on a door step. She thought he was hiding when the blood spilled all over him. He had been shot in the face.

Further up the road the bulldozers' teeth have razed to the ground the houses in an entire street; it was too narrow for the tanks so they made room for them. The demolition of dozens of houses began on Saturday, April 6, four days after the IDF invaded Jenin. It is not yet possible to know how many people were trapped under the debris but local people feared that entire families were buried alive.

Widely expected, the attack began on the night of Tuesday April 2; the scout raised the alarm, the children threw stones on empty barrels to 'scare' the tanks, families had been evacuated.

For two days IDF artillery shelled the refugee camp from all directions; water and electricity supplies were cut off in the first hours of the attack. Two days later, the shooting from helicopters, often operating in pairs, began in a blaze of fire. It barely stopped during the next four days; during one attack, eyewitnesses counted over 400 missiles fired in less than four hours. Using a satellite, the IDF had outlined in red the positions of 1,100 houses. The helicopter pilots got a random number and opened fire.

Forced home by the military curfew, people found shelter under staircases, crowded into small rooms for entire days, in darkness, cuddling the small children while everything around them was tumbling down. From a population of 14,000 people, four to five thousand refused to leave their homes and remained there.

In the ruined camp there was a block of bricked-up houses which was engulfed in flames. One of the dwellings had been spared by the fire and in the two rooms, both pierced with cannonades, bits of human flesh are still on the walls. Beside them a child's drawing was stuck on a door, miraculously intact. According to one neighbour, someone from the family who lived there survived the Apache's rockets but a foot patrol passing by blew off the door and threw hand grenades into the house, leaving no survivors. It is no surprise then, if last Friday a young woman from the camp strapped explosives under her shirt and blew herself up beside a bus in West Jerusalem.[1]

Children are using their bare hands to search in the rubble, trying to rescue something from the ruins: a jumper, a car tyre, anything. A distressed woman takes my hand, bringing me into a shabby house which was raked by Israeli missiles. In a room there are three bodies lying on the floor; they are unrecognizable, blackened, swollen. Fat flies fill the rays of light filtering from the holes made by the rockets. One body is deformed and bent on himself; his arms are open like Christ on the Cross and his mouth, open wide, is filled with creepy-crawlies, his teeth as white as snow contrasting against his dark face. A page from an Arab paper covers the worst injury. The smell of decay is so atrocious that it makes it hard to breathe; worms are crawling everywhere. Another body in the corner is decapitated but the head is nowhere to be seen. The woman takes off the quilt which has covered up her eyes; she sits down, throws dust all over her head and starts crying.

On approaching the district right in the centre of the camp, the silence is deafening. Scaring the hell out of us, a cat scampers over rocks and bricks, clearly disorientated. Echoes of laments and screaming make the place even more frightening.

Wrapped in white plastic shrouds and blankets four corpses were piled up around the corner, as if they were bags of food left lying outside a closed shop. But they are human beings still. We are told they are waiting for the IDF to allow their removal. All

Aerial photographs taken by the IDF showing the destruction in the heart of Jenin refugee camp. The one at the top was taken on April 11, the day after armed resistance had ceased. The other one, dated April 13, was taken before the caterpillars flattened 'Jeningrad' into a compressed expanse of rubble.

Top: A house on the edge between Jenin city and its refugee camp.
Bottom: Life around 'Ground Zero'.

Top: A woman in what once was her house. The upper floor no longer exists. *Bottom:* The ruins of 'Jeningrad', the Hanat al Hawashin district of the city.

Jenin: a woman stands at the door of her house surrounded by destruction. She can't get out as she is ill and the steps have been flattened by the huge D-9 bulldozers.

around, rushing from the top of the camp, streams of dirty water carry away the debris in the tracks dug out by the bulldozers.

During the invasion IDF soldiers advanced from house to house, making large holes in the walls to enter the next home, officially to avoid the risks of Palestinian gunmen. An old man insists on showing me what remains of his house, compressed in a sculpture of mutilated iron arms and twisted metal. His sister lives next door; a bulldozer knocked a lamp pole over the detached building; she claims that was a way to 'mark' the target for the Apache which then fired two missiles into it. The house appears curiously solid from the outside while inside it looks like a tornado had passed through it.

The sound of a child screaming for help takes me back on to the street. He has just found a human leg in the debris and there is only one person around. An old man lifts him in his arms, calming him down gently before his mother returns. How could anyone possibly do this to children? What have they done to them? Will it ever be possible to persuade them 'not to transform their grief into a tool of hatred but into foundations for change'?

Someone else points to what had previously been a house where two sisters lived. Neighbours say they were crippled. It is still unknown whether they are under the ruins or if they got out of the camp in time. In the next room, there are two wounded people, bleeding copiously and screaming for help; the air is saturated with the smell of burning flesh, body parts are stuck on the walls, insects everywhere.

An old grey house barely stands on its own skeleton; burnt pages from the Koran and a shoe are visible in the middle of the rubble. Graffiti glorifying the 'Jihad', the holy war, are fading from a wall sprayed with 50mm gun-fire.

Death and destruction are everywhere. Another small child walks me to his aunt, climbing up and down heaps of rubbish and making his way between piles of cement. The woman was hit in the abdomen by a dum-dum bullet only three days ago. She is shivering in a pool of blood; no doctor can get to her and she is dying. Her daughters are crying in the corner. But there is no time to bring her any help. Somebody shouts in Arabic and without saying a word, the child pulls me to the back of the house and into a backyard. An IDF foot patrol is in the area and about 15 people hide between the concrete pillars and the collapsed ceilings.

I follow a local man into a dark lane when, all of the sudden, we emerge into the heart of the refugee camp. It was a neighbourhood known as Hanat al Hawashin. It no longer exists.

Around the central ruins a ring of half-wrecked houses has survived the seismic tremors. It looks like the place had been hit by an earthquake. My eyes have never seen anything like this before. From here I can see at least two or three hundred square metres of a densely populated area, in some cases three-storey buildings, turned into a wild expanse of rubble and dust. It resembles a moonscape; it is a ground zero, like a huge tomb.

After been fired upon by the Apache and Cobra helicopter gunships, the district was left to the IDF caterpillars which drove over the piles of cement several times, grounding everything to dust. Walking on the top of the flattened houses is distressing; until a few days ago hundreds of people, families, children lived here. There was life under my feet; now there might be murdered kids and entombed disabled people.

The unbearable stench of dead bodies mingles with the surprising smells of geranium, roses and mint cultivated at the edge of the camp. Challenging the curfew, the locals who fled the brunt of the attack are now starting to return but they cannot find their houses; they have lost everything. They walk over their pulverised district, which was home for about 800 Palestinian families, numbed, paralysed.

A woman in a long satin dress explains:

> Israeli soldiers took a four month old baby from her father's arms and ordered him to walk, along with his own father, into a narrow alleyway. The IDF asked them to pull up their shirts and then sprayed them with bullets; saved by the body of his son falling on him, the old man survived, pretending to be dead until the soldiers had gone and crawled to safety. They were our neighbours.

> My own family is dispersed. Look around you, look at what they have done to us. Tell everyone; you must tell the whole world what they have done to us.

A dusty doll is trapped between sharp and twisted iron bars; an old woman suggests there is no point in trying to pull it out because its three year old owner has probably been killed, by machine-gun bursts, days before the bulldozer razed the area to the ground. The smell of rotting human corpses reeks from underneath the havoc. Nobody knows how many people could be buried there. New dead bodies are being discovered every day.

After a few minutes people start running away as Israeli armoured vehicles come roaring in our direction. We buy a few minutes by retreating back into the maze of narrow lanes but by now troops are in control of the area. Along with other journalists and local people we are escorted by the tanks out of the camp and towards the city hospital.

Outside the hospital, itself besieged by the tanks, nurses have sprayed dead bodies with perfume to make the job less awful; the bodies have been placed in temporary mass graves by the doctors, without any religious ceremony.

A young nurse points to large craters left as a result of the explosions which happened the day 13 soldiers had been killed. For revenge the Israelis bombed the hospital and the ambulances.[2]

Throughout the IDF incursion medics and ambulance crews were constantly fired upon. One nurse was murdered while attempting to retrieve the body of a young girl. Medical staff were prevented from reaching the wounded in a calculated policy that meant they would bleed to death.

More injured people are arriving at the hospital, but a line of tanks and troops prevents them from reaching it. IDF fire continues at intervals, though there are no longer any Palestinians left to shoot at the soldiers. The heart brims over with anger and helplessness, silently weeping in the unreal, deafening and desperate silence of death.

The view from the Baraha primary school: a small section of Hanat al Hawashin, the outskirts of the city and the expanses leading to the Lebanon border.

Notes

1. Two people and the bomber were killed in the attack. She was the fourth female martyr since Wafa Idris, 28, from Ramallah, blew herself up in Jerusalem's Jaffa Street on January 27. The other two, 21-year old Danin Aysheh and Ayat Akhras (18), both from the refugee camps outside Bethlehem, were responsible for the death of five Israelis between February and March 2002. There have been cases in which women led the revolution from the front, even hijacking planes (Leila Khaled), but there had never been a suicide bomber before. While the use of girls for such missions marks a stark switch of tactics, probably even more alarming is the development in suicide bombing overall. At the beginning of the uprising a martyr would have been young, unmarried, desperate, fanatically religious and thus susceptible to Islam's promise of a 'shaheed', a place in paradise. Today's bomber no longer fits the profile. Daoud Abu Sway, a 47-year old father of eight, detonated the bomb which killed three people and himself in a Jerusalem hotel. Izadin Masri was the owner of a prosperous food chain, yet he killed 15 people in Jerusalem's Sbarro Restaurant.
2. Some of the Israeli soldiers killed in the ambush were originally either Russians or Druse. Thus the IDF has been accused of sending 'foreign' troops into particularly risky situations.

3.

The eye witnesses

'The Israeli authorities may well be able to hide the evidence but they cannot silence the stories that are pouring out from those who evaded the killings', claims Dr Zaid from Jenin hospital, describing how many people have been killed or maimed by helicopter missiles and machine-gun fire.

It is only one of the harrowing testimonies from the 'slaughterhouse', as it was described by some foreign media. It is still a very early stage but the tales of horror and the testimonies of dozens of witnesses seem entirely consistent with each other on the extent and the types of abuses that were carried out in the camp.

Strong suspicious are raised by a young doctor – Abu is his name – who wonders

> why here at the hospital or in the camp itself, no seriously injured people were found, only the walking wounded. We ask the Israeli government to disclose where the seriously wounded are and also where are the bodies of all those killed in Jenin.

Eye witnesses provide their own explanation. They have seen the IDF digging mass graves, bulldozing the dead bodies into the sewage system, burning them, booby-trapping them, spiriting them away in big army lorries. Many reports claim the corpses of the Palestinian fighters were taken to a secret location in the Jordan Valley and buried in a special cemetery used by the Israelis to hide embarrassing evidence: terrorists or enemy forces.

Hiding the bodies of those he slaughtered was what Slobodan Milosevic did in Bosnia and Kosovo. But the former Serbian leader is on trial in the Hague for war crimes while Sharon is labelled 'a man of peace' by American president G.W. Bush.[1]

Having walked the camp's streets, it appears obvious why the media and human rights groups have been kept away from Jenin for so many days and why, as the Tel Aviv media report, the IDF was running out of body bags.

According to local people not all the civilians were cut down in crossfire as claimed by the Israeli authorities. Fourteen year old Ahmed fled the camp

> when the helicopters rained a hurricane of missiles. We ran to safety, my mother and my small brothers, but we didn't know about my father. I came back to the house but there's no more house. I've heard hundreds of people have been arrested; I hope my father is with them, not under the ruins of our home. The woman who lived next door says she heard grenades and shooting from where my father was hiding. But I know he is still alive.

Abu Rashid and other members of his family ran out of the house with their hands up, yelling at the bulldozer driver that there were people inside. His son Jamal, 35, is confined to a wheelchair. The huge vehicle did not stop roaring; it retreated a bit and then attacked again, in front of their eyes; in less than two minutes the concrete wall came falling down on Jamal.

In a very similar incident Ibrahim succeeded in alerting a bulldozer driver that people were in a house that was about to be demolished. 'The IDF listened to him, they even thanked him; they turned their mechanical monsters and drove away. But a soldier came out of a tank. We saw him grab the machine gun and knock Ibrahim down with a short burst',[2] proclaims a woman in a file compiled by the Israeli human rights group B'Tselem.

According to an old man,

> many people were too terrified to leave the basement where they had found shelter. The family of a local school teacher was among them. Now I've heard they are all dead, parents and five children; they say the soldiers didn't bother to issue a warning; they just drove over them.

People recall an IDF patrol which forced children to knock walls and doors down. Before the patrol was replaced they allegedly took the children to an alleyway and shot them dead. The bodies were then thrown on the road and crushed by tanks.

A systematic pattern of human rights abuses and war crimes is clearly beginning to emerge. 'The bodies of about 30 people, only a few of them armed militants, were thrown into the ruins of a wrecked house and one Merkava drove over them two or three times', maintains Abu, who fought with the PLO in the past.

In the stories from the refugee camp's inferno – 'Jeningrad', as the Palestinians have renamed the area around the centre of the camp – memories are revisited like nightmares; people find it hard to remember exact dates; all the days of the assault have become a tangle of fear, blood and devastation, without any nights or days. Many families have spent much of the last three weeks hidden and isolated in their houses. Their accounts of events are often confused and sometimes they have no idea of what was happening in the camp.

For more than two weeks without water or electricity, many refugees were forced to eat leaves from the trees, search in the rubbish for food and drink contaminated water from the sewers. Appalling sanitary conditions and decomposed bodies may trigger epidemics and quickly spread infections, especially among the children and the elderly.

Like many others, Abu Riyad, 51 years old, was enlisted for IDF missions. For five days he was forced to accompany the soldiers from door to door while troops concealed themselves behind him. At the end of one mission they handcuffed him and told him to stay inside a certain house, knowing all too well the tanks were about to demolish it. On seeing the tanks coming, Abu jumped from house to house until he got to his home. As soon as he was inside, a Cobra helicopter fired eight rockets, allegedly killing 13 people.

Amer al-Karim, aged 24 states:

> Israeli soldiers would have us walk in front of them, sometimes with them resting their rifles on our shoulders. At times they were exchanging gunfire and shooting from people's shoulders.

Different eye-witnesses confirm that an IDF patrol had recruited a young Palestinian.

The fighting was still going on and the soldiers were having a break in a derelict house. One of them had forgotten his skull cap in a house they had just searched and told the young boy that if he brought him back the skull cap he would be released. The boy ran to the house, brought the skull cap back and was allowed to go home.

According to local people the IDF left live grenades beside dead bodies, shot dead a young and mentally disabled boy waving a white flag from his wheelchair and fired indiscriminately at civilians.

In a chilly reminder of old tragedies, after the mass arrests in Jenin the soldiers separated the men from the women before loading them onto lorries to deport them. IDF soldiers defecated inside the mosque and desecrated holy books. Israeli sources claim that approximately 200 tanks and between 7,000 and 10,000 IDF soldiers were involved in the offensive.

Amnesty International was the first official humanitarian body to issue a strongly worded report.

It is almost impossible to conceive that what once was a town has now been transformed into a lunar landscape. If this had been an earthquake the international community would be asked for and give urgent help. It is shocking that the authorities have not asked for help and that the international community has not offered it.

The report traces credible claims of basic human rights and international humanitarian law violations, including:

Failure to give civilians warnings or time to evacuate the refugee camp before the helicopters launched their strike; allegations of extra-judicial executions; failure to allow a 14 days long humanitarian assistance period to the people enclosed into the camp; denial of medical assistance and deliberate targeting of Red Cross and Red Crescent personnel; excessive use of lethal force and the usage of civilians as human shields; ill-treatment, including torture and degrading treatment, of Palestinian detainees; excessive damage to property with no apparent military necessity.

According to the refugees who lived here, there were between 200 and 500 'Fedayeen' defending the camp; they were from Hamas, Islamic Jihad and the al-Aqsa Brigades, fighting alongside PNA security forces, mostly armed with Kalashnikovs and explosives. But anyone who helped them saw themselves as active in the resistance; locals say that no door in the camp was closed to them when they had to face helicopters and tanks.

The Palestinian resistance shocked the IDF which had previously predicted a swift victory because of its overwhelming superiority in armaments. 'We were not expecting them to fight so well', admitted an army officer to Israeli Radio.

Militant leaders inside the camp were prepared for the Israeli invasion and having studied previous IDF incursions, they were able to predict how and when the troops would be deployed. After the bombing in Netanya the calls came from the mosque to be prepared for the enemy. Bomb-makers manufactured devices, snipers took up positions, tunnels were dug to gain some freedom of movement, ambush plans were put in motion. Ordinary citizens also took up arms to defend their homes, despite knowing that it was in vain.

From the first reconstruction it appears that after four days of shelling and bombing the army tried to get the infantry into the camp. But because of armed resistance the plan failed; 13 army reservists died in an ambush while suicide bombers ran toward the tanks to delay their offensive. 'It was after that they started to attack all the houses in the camp with helicopters and tanks, indiscriminately', people agree.

Despite the huge disproportion of firepower they resisted for eight days before gradually being pushed deeper into the heart of the camp, to their last battle, where ground zero now stands.

Some 36 guerrillas surrendered on Thursday – after running out of ammunition according to the Israelis, to evacuate a group of women and children threatened by the Merkavas, according to the Palestinians.

The army replied to the white flags with tank shelling, allegedly killing two and wounding several. The bulk of the fighters, and we might never know exactly how many there were, have been lost.

The invasion is not even over and Jenin is already a battle scream. It has entered the collective memory of the Arab world, is a new symbol of resistance; in Gaza and the West Bank mothers are naming their new born babies after the martyred city.

Through the Defensive Shield operation Sharon may have well wiped out hundreds of militants but how many new martyrs has he created?

When I attempt to return to Jenin, I find that all the possible routes, including via Salem, are blocked by the army. At the checkpoint a column of tanks is rumbling out of a thick cloud of dust and sand.

Behind the Merkavas, in an armoured car, Terje Larsen, United Nations special envoy for the Middle East, is just returning from the camp.[3] For 18 days the IDF did everything humanly possible to keep indiscreet and inquisitive eyes away from Jenin and this is the first time they allowed a UN team in.

Larsen appears shaken.

> The world has underestimated the scale of what happened here. Nobody knows how many people could be buried underneath the rubble. It's horrifying beyond belief. Whatever was the objective of the military operation, the means were totally disproportionate and morally unjustifiable.

Notes

1. The US president made the unfortunate comment on April 16, in other words when the first reports on the scale of death and destruction in the camp were already in the public domain.
2 . Source: B'Tselem.
3. In the early 1990s, while working in Gaza for a Norwegian institute, Larsen had acted as a mediator in the first approach between Palestinians and Israelis; these resulted in the 1991 Madrid peace-talks, which led to the Oslo Agreement.

4.

Jenin's voices

Reem Saleh celebrated her 15th birthday two days before the IDF attacked the refugee camp where she lived. Before the ordeal she wanted to be a teacher. 'Now I want to be a martyr; all of my friends want to be martyrs', she wrote.

As a gift for her birthday her father, Jamal, gave Reem a pen. The small object survived searches and raids and along with a small radio became her only link with what her life used to be and with the outside world.

The Saleh family was lucky because their house was chosen to have an IDF sniper's emplacement on its roof and so was not destroyed like the buildings around it. Reem's diary starts on April 3.

First day

I hear tanks and helicopters. The Israeli troops have entered Jenin city. All day the muezzin from the mosque is calling out for resistance. 'Calling all Palestinians, Hamas, Fatah, Jihad. Resist the army. We are on alert!'

By Saturday they have entered the camp, moving slowly. They have confined the camp, circled it. There are so many tanks, especially in the Jabriat and Saadeh areas and there has been fighting all day between the Palestinian resistance and the Israeli army. So many houses have already been taken over and families are scattered. Snipers are everywhere now, posted inside the houses, especially in the Jabriat area.

The resistance tried to stop the army from taking the camp and six Palestinians were killed as well as two

Israeli soldiers. That's what the Israeli radio reports. The
resistance said Israelis will take the camp only over our
dead bodies. They used RPGs for the first time and three
Israeli tanks were destroyed. The resistance leaders say
there are a lot of surprises in store for the Israelis.

Saturday April 6, 9.30 am

Israeli troops broke into our house and took over the
rooms. We heard their voices outside the house. They
broke furniture and seem very angry. They are rubbing
dark camouflage cream on their faces. Some were
nervous and I could see the hatred in their eyes. One of
the soldiers spat on us. Then some soldiers took my father
into a room, using him as a shield while they were
shooting out from holes they made in the walls.

When one entered the room, he pushed everything aside
with the end of his gun, knocking things off shelves and
everything is broken. They moved all 24 – neighbours,
cousins and relatives – into my uncle Sophi's room. I still
can't believe they are in my house. I feel nothing, numb.
We all raised our hands in the air when they came in so
they wouldn't shoot.

All day there was sounds of explosions, Kalashnikov
and M16s from our side. From the Israelis, there is the
sound of helicopters overhead, all day long. I am scared.
I hear tanks firing. I can hear planes, F16s in the sky.

My little brothers and my cousins are hiding. When we
look out of the window we see tanks, army vehicles and
bulldozers pushing over houses. We see people leaving
their houses with their hands up.

Sunday April 7

An Israeli soldier was shot in our house. He was seriously
injured. There is blood all over his face and he is
screaming. The other soldiers put bandages on his face
and his arm; they put a drip with glucose in his arm. He
screams for his mother.

I am afraid they will take revenge. They scream at us in Hebrew. They tell us not to go near the window. One soldier is so angry that he bangs his head against the wall.

The Apache shells the camp all day and the soldier tells us, 'We will not leave this place until all the armed men surrender'. The Palestinian resistance pledged not to. The muezzin from the mosque continues all day, telling fighters to resist. There is only one left who works in the camp but he keeps telling them to resist.

Monday April 8

Today, Israeli reports say two soldiers were killed and five injured. There are 50 Palestinians killed.

Palestinian sources are different. They say there are hundreds of Palestinians killed. The radio also says there is a massacre here in the camp and the world knows nothing about it.

The Apache keeps shelling. The houses are burning. No one knows how many people have died in their houses. Today there is heavy fighting in Nablus, where my uncle and aunt live...

Our neighbours live across the road. They have sent the children to our house to be safe but the parents are staying because they don't want to leave the house. The house gets rocketed and the parents move to the first floor. Then the second floor gets hit again by a rocket and they finally move out. Now they only have half a house.

All the children here heard the rockets and are scared. When the Apaches circle above us the children put their hands over their ears and the Israelis tell them not to be afraid. 'They know we are here; you won't get rocketed', they say.

Tuesday April 9

I watched Israeli soldiers demolish a house with a bulldozer. I see Palestinian people coming out of the house with their hands up but I can't see their faces.

A pregnant neighbour called Hyam comes knocking at our door. She is having pains and she is frightened. The soldiers scream at her to go away but she has nowhere to go. She is pushed out on the street holding her little daughter who is waving a white cloth, like a flag. But they shoot at them anyway.

Hyam is not hurt but she is scared. When she gets back to her demolished house, her husband is gone. He has been arrested by the Israelis. Her other children were taken by her neighbour.

Wednesday April 10

There is a radio report of a suicide bomber in Haifa, on a bus. He came from Jenin.

Thursday April 11

I listen to the radio which says that the Israelis demolished ten houses. There are fighters inside those houses. Inside our house we have read the Koran. We can't change or wash our clothes so we wear the same ones everyday.

The children have to stay quiet or the soldiers yell at them, sometimes for hours and hours, only to traumatise them.

Friday April 12

Another suicide bomber in Jerusalem. Every day is the same. I have heard that 13 soldiers have died in the Jenin camp. I don't know where it is because there are explosions all the time. The soldiers get very angry and one of them tells my father: 'Now we will not leave until every Arab is dead.'[1]

Reem escaped the mass arrests, the destruction of houses and the executions, but for her and other such children childhood ended abruptly. They have been exposed to both physical and psychological violence which goes beyond their endurance.

Palestinian children, when arrested, are subjected to the same level of torture, cruelty, inhuman and degrading punishment as adults. They are being deliberately killed by bullets and by the economic apartheid which targets the most vulnerable levels of Palestinian society. More than 7,000 have already been injured or maimed by Israeli soldiers or settlers. According to UNICEF's Jerusalem office 600,000 Palestinian children are currently unable to attend school due to bombing or restriction of movement.

> When we got into the camp, the D9s (military bulldozers) were already waiting. First thing I did was to tie the Beitar (Israeli football team) flag to the bulldozer. I wanted my family to be able to identify me. I told my family and my kids, 'You'll see my tractor on television. When you see the Beitar flag, that will be me.

This chilling tale of those days is told by a young Israeli, Moshe Nissim, who drove one of the IDF bulldozers during the Israeli invasion of Jenin.

> Do you know how I held out for 75 hours of straight bulldozing? I didn't get off the tractor. I had no problem of fatigue, because I drank whiskey all the time. I had bottles in the tractor at all times. For three days I destroyed and destroyed. The whole area. Any house that they fired from came down. And to knock it down, I tore down some more.
>
> The Palestinians were warned by loud speakers to get out of their homes before I came, but I gave no one a chance. I did not wait for them to come out. I would just ram the house with full power, to bring it down as fast as possible. I wanted to get to the other houses, to get as many as possible. Others may have restrained themselves, or so they say. Who are they kidding?
>
> I am sure people died inside these houses, but it was difficult to see. There was lots of dust everywhere and we worked a lot at night. I found joy with every house that came down, because I knew that they didn't mind dying, but they cared for their homes. If you knocked down a house, you buried 40 or 50 people for generations. If I am sorry for anything it is not tearing the whole camp down.'[2]

The D-9's unit operating in Jenin received a medal for 'distinction in battle'; that happened on the very same day the UN was forced to renounce the investigation into the events in Jenin.

Even the Israeli Attorney General's office has admitted that in some cases houses were demolished before their Palestinian inhabitants had moved out. On April 6, in Nablus, a house in the casbah was bulldozed by the IDF on top of ten members of the al-Shu'bi family. Eight were killed, including three children, their pregnant mother and 85 year-old grandfather.

A woman walks through the debris in the Jenin refugee camp, recites the writer Tahar Ben Jelloun in his latest book, *Jenin, un campo palestinese*.

Where am I? An obsession of mine to ask myself where I am all the time. I've never had much sense of direction; but then, the question meant something elsewhere. Here who would be able to tell me the name of this place of ruin, this place unlike any other. A place of the void, perhaps, at the back of the desert, the end of the city…?

My eyes betray me. I can see, I can't see. What I see no longer exists…Why all these flies? They are big and tacky. A dead cat? No, it's not a cat, an old discarded doll, lying there. Bleeding. Weeping. In any case I don't want to play with dolls, not at my age. But I'm no longer any age. I've been confiscated.

It's amazing what you can find under stones. A key. An old key. It's big. What does it open? Perhaps it's the key to Paradise? I'll keep it. I'll put it in my pocket just in case my feet should slip towards the gates of Paradise.

I'm not thirsty any more. I'm not hungry any more. I'm looking for my home. This stone is from the side wall of my house. I recognise it. It's not like the others. I'll keep it. Hide it under my feet. No one shall take it from me. It's my stone, a tiny corner of my home. I'll plant it by and by. It'll give me a tree, the tree will give me shade and I'll live beneath my tree.

The woman sitting among the ruins finds a photograph and looks at it.

I know this man, I've seen him before. The girls no, I don't know them. Will all these people come back? All? And the dead? Those swallowed up by the debris? They will come to put their houses back together. Their home is everywhere, anywhere now. Scattered. I will help them. We'll gather stone after stone and build the walls.

The sun is hurting me. It's mocking my eyes. It shows me groups of houses, then makes them tumble like a pack of cards. They fall quickly. A cloud of dust rises or falls, I don't know any more. Some of these clouds of dust remain suspended in mid-air. If it rains, the rain will be black.

My eyes are still moving, they are speaking, telling me that the whole neighbourhood has been razed to the ground, yes, destroyed. They love to destroy, it's their job, to destroy, demolish, sweep away, annihilate. They sought out the men and killed them. That's what they did.

I remember. The images return in procession, visit me to prevent death from overwhelming everything. I remember this huge machine advancing in the night, destroying all in its path. Soldiers shooting. They were frightened. They killed men, children, cats. They say they're after terrorists.

What does this debris correspond to? Before them, before the howling and the bodies riddled with bullets, before the faces, the backs – straight or bent – what was there here? A kind of life. One waited. One hoped. From the camp one hoped to move to a real city, a simple proper life, no glitter but no howling.

There are no ruins; there's my house, the carpenter's shop, the fountain and above all the tree which gives me shade. It's all there in my head, in my heart, in this dust which witnesses and accuses, even if all is arranged so that the debris is illegible. The crime is there, although covered with tons of debris and silence. The crime has been buried. Buried in the same bed as the dead.

They have destroyed the tombs. The dead have re-awoken; they haunt them in their sleep. I can sleep no more, eat no more, drink no more. I am a stone, the oldest, the most resistant. I can speak. I can tell. Nothing shall keep me silent. Nothing shall break me. Nothing shall shift me. The soldiers have gone. Some in plastic bags. I am waiting. I am not weeping. I cannot weep. My heart is dry. Dry as a stone. And yet I have many tears to shed. I am unable to do so.

Some people come to count the dead. They call out at random where the survivors should be. How can you count what have been mangled? You must first gather the torn limbs together, recompose the bodies and then count.

The cannons are thundering, the machine-guns are shooting, the loudspeakers are blaring, the sound of the siren of an ambushed ambulance can be heard. The driver is dead, the injured will have all night to die. The ambulance is another bombed house, another felled tree; the tree has lost its branches and the birds have been carbonised by the fire of the weapons, the fire of men who tremble with hatred.

I will stay here, seated, forever, unchanging until the fall of the moon. It will come down to fetch us because our need of justice is great, violent like the advancing desert. It is our history which bleeds, not our hearts or our eyes.

Uri Avnery writes:

One hundred and five years ago, the day after the First Zionist Congress in Basel, Theodor Herzi wrote in his diary: "In Basel I founded the state of the Jews". This week Ariel Sharon should note in his diary: "In Jenin I founded the state of the Palestinians".

According to the Israeli writer, peace activist and former member of the Tel Aviv government, 'it all goes back to 1967. In these years the form of occupation may have changed but the content has remained the same. It is this contest that lies at the heart of the conflict'.

Israel as a whole did not question Jenin until Uri Avnery's condemnation of his government policy.

Faced with the onslaught of the biggest military machine in the region and the most modern arms in the world, submerged in a sea of suffering, surrounded by bodies, the Palestinian nation straightened its back as never before.

Jenin child.

In the small refugee camp near Jenin a group of Palestinian fighters from all the organizations gathered for a battle of defence that will be enshrined forever in the hearts of all Arabs.

When the international media cannot be kept out anymore and the pictures of horror are published, two possible versions may emerge: Jenin as a story of massacre, a second Sabra and Chatila; and Jenin, a Palestinian Stalingrad of immortal heroism, which will surely prevail. Nations are built on myths. The myths of Jenin and Arafat's compound in Ramallah will form the consciousness of the new Palestinian nation.

As for the actual forces, the balance is clear: a few dozen Israelis killed, many hundreds of Palestinians dead. No destruction in Israel, horrible devastation in the Palestinian towns.

The aim was, so it was claimed, to 'destroy the terror infrastructure'. This definition is nonsensical; the 'terror infrastructure' exists in the souls of millions of Palestinians and tens of millions of Arabs whose hearts are bursting with rage.

When dozens of wounded people lie around in the streets and slowly bleed to death because the army shoots at every moving ambulance, it creates terrible hatred. When the army secretly buries hundreds of bodies of men, women and children it creates terrible hatred. When tanks run over cars, destroy houses, topple electricity poles, open water pipes, leave behind them thousands of homeless people and cause children to drink from puddles in the streets, it creates terrible hatred.

A Palestinian child who sees all this with his eyes, becomes the suicide bomber of tomorrow. Thus Sharon and Mofaz[3] create the terrorist infrastructure.

In the meantime they have created the foundations of the Palestinian nation and the Palestinian state. The people saw their fighters in Jenin and believe that they are far greater heroes than the Israeli soldiers, protected as they are inside their heavy tanks. They saw their leader in the historic tv sequences, his face lighted by a single candle in his office, ready for death at any moment. National pride is engendered.

No good for Israel will come out of this adventure, as no good came out of the previous adventures of Sharon. The concept of the operation was stupid, the implementation cruel; the results will be disastrous. It will not bring peace and security, solve no problem, but it will isolate Israel and endanger Jews throughout the world.

In the end, only one thing will be remembered: our giant military machine assaulted the small Palestinian people, and the small Palestinian people and its leader held on. In the eyes of the Palestinians, and not only theirs, it will look like a tremendous victory.[4]

Notes

1. Source: *Indymedia*, April 20, 2002.
2. Source: *Yediot Ahoronot*, May 31, 2002.
3. Shaul Mofaz, Commander in Chief of the Israeli armed forces, together with Benyamin Ben Eliezer, the Labour Party's Defence Minister (who is said to have been involved in the massacre of hundreds of captured Egyptian soldiers after they had surrendered in the Sinai Desert), along with Prime Minister Ariel Sharon are responsible for the IDF's military operations in this latest Intifada.
4. Source: *Indymedia* April 19, 2002.

A disabled child from the Gaza City refugee camp. The special school
for disabled, run by the UN, was destroyed during an Apache attack.

5.

The IDF

The crime perpetrated in Jenin is not just the nastiest act in Sharon's vicious war on terrorism since his election. The plan had long languished on his desk and because Operation Defensive Shield was to become the largest military offensive since the 1967 war, Jenin was very high in the list of targets.

In December 2001, the 'plan' drawn up by Sharon at the time of his election was officially made public. It was a very simple plot: eradicating the Palestinians from the Territories by exterminating them, bombing the refugee camps and gradually reoccupying the West Bank and Gaza, exiling the survivors east of the River Jordan, annexing the Territories to Israel and de facto erasing Palestine from the map.

Having seen the plunder of Jenin, the plan looks at an advanced stage and there is nothing to derail it. Further surprises could also be on the cards: some are inspired by the extreme right wingers in Sharon's Likud Party who advocate a form of 'transfer', the mass expulsion of the one million Palestinians, labelled as 'a cancer', who are citizens of Israel itself. 'The second half of 1948', in the words of Israeli generals.

Back at the Salem checkpoint, the containers for dead Palestinians are still here, surrounded by the Merkavas impaired during the battle. The Israeli Army is a highly organized military organization; an ice-cream van and an itinerant synagogue on a bus are parked among the tanks to offer relief to the distressed troops returning for Jenin. A few yards away military policemen are taking the handcuffs off four young Palestinians, who are released and start walking home toward Jenin with tanks passing by them.[1]

The last time we were here we had to challenge the third most powerful armed organization in the world in our attempt to reach

Jenin. Today it is the IDF itself that offers us a lift. They vehemently deny a massacre has taken place in Jenin and they are extremely keen to prove it. Escorted by tanks, two buses loaded with journalists enter the closed military zone, stopping beside artillery positions overlooking the camp for a military briefing.

'You can all see Jenin still stands behind me', declares Colonel Miri Esen proudly, gesturing to the city behind her.

> The camp doesn't look great. We are not denying that the centre of the camp was destroyed. But it was not a massacre, only the result of the heaviest urban fighting we have seen for 30 years. The battle was fierce because we sought to minimize civilian casualties. We might have called the F16 jetfighters and only one bomb would have done the whole job. Instead, we sent in the infantry.

The senior intelligence officer claims that 25 Palestinian bodies, of which four were wearing explosive belts used by suicide bombers, have so far been recovered and only two of them are civilians.

> Only a hundred houses have been destroyed but one of the goals of this whole operation was the destruction of the terrorist infrastructure. We have protected the civilian population after the militants booby-trapped the camp.

To the Israelis, 'Jenin is the suicide bombers' capital, the cobra-head of Palestinian terrorism. Since the start of the Intifada, 28 martyrs, mainly from Hamas and the Islamic Jihad, came from here,' Colonel Esen explains before citing historical metaphors. 'Jenin was the Palestinian Masada, like the suicidal last stand of Jewish warriors besieged by Roman invaders in their hilltop fortress in AD 73.'

Also present at the briefing is Brigadier General Eyal Shlein, divisional commander for operations in the Jenin area. Speaking in Hebrew beside a display of aerial photographs, he tries to reassure us that 'civilians were given proper warning and asked to surrender; some of them have not'. Quoting his own premier, Shlein believes that his 'soldiers showed restraint while operating in a very difficult territory. There would have been no problem completing the operation immediately, but we are a humane army'.

The IDF suffered 23 casualties and more than a hundred soldiers were wounded in Jenin.[2] Usually Israel's retaliation for a similar death toll would be much higher than 'just' killing 25 Palestinians.

Ariel Sharon launches a huge public relations drive to counter the timid international backlash and conceal the truth about Jenin. Everyone else seems guilty apart from the Israelis. The government claimed the army acted to protect ordinary Palestinians but it is hard to deny that in such a densely populated area civilian casualties could not have been prevented.

Tel Aviv lashes out at the International Red Cross, whose ambulances were fired upon, accusing them of smuggling weapons and carrying out fighters posing as injured people. The IRC dismissed the claims as 'nonsense', describing the ban on ambulances and medical assistance, which openly violates the Geneva Convention, as 'unacceptable'.

Attacking the media for 'exaggerating the reports', the IDF declared that ground zero is merely an area of about a hundred square metres, when in reality it is the size of two or three football pitches. They claimed to have demolished only 100 houses but the first reports indicate the real number may be three times higher. Yet, the bottom line remains the same. No conceivable military reason can justify such devastation.

Israeli officials blamed UNWRA[3] for allowing 'terrorist infrastructures to develop' in the camp without raising any alarm. UNWRA officials wearily point out that it does not administer the camp but only provides services like schools and clinics.

IDF spokespersons stated that the army bulldozed the buildings only after the battle ended, largely because they were heavily booby-trapped. They argued that the Palestinians blew up their own camp, compelling the army to level it. While it is impossible to establish how many booby-traps were hidden around the camp, there is little doubt that this is a device frequently used by a retreating force against an advancing one. Here the Palestinian fighters had nowhere to go.

'The IDF has nothing to fear' from the fact-finding mission proposed by the United Nations, declares the Prime Minister; the cover-up will eventually protect the army and the state.

There is a strong suspicion that the IDF soldiers were given a green light to do everything necessary to curb the resistance in Jenin. In two separate incidents at the end of April seven children were wounded by the explosion of land mines in Nablus and Jenin, allegedly left by the humane army before leaving the camp.

Some of these soldiers did what they did from sheer hate, some from sadism, the vast majority because of fear. Whatever the reasons though they all feed the same cycle of endless attacks and reprisals. IDF atrocities and Palestinian armed resistance proceed symmetrically; they run parallel and obtain the same result. Terrorism on Israeli civilians must be condemned and rejected, yet the condemnation should also include the policies that directly produced terrorism in the first place. Here only one side is blamed for being terrorist. From this particular angle the two factions act in the very same way, but with a massive disparity of might – sling-shots against tanks.

It should not be forgotten that military service is compulsory in Israel; after their terms of conscription, 36 and 24 months long for boys and girls respectively, every Israeli is recalled to serve as a reservist for about two months every year, until the age of 50. There is certainly some truth in saying that an Israeli is a life-time soldier with a ten-month annual leave.

Recently, however, IDF reservists attracted much political attention by refusing to serve in the Occupied Territories. A small army of peace, 53 soldiers and officers, some from the elite units which usually carry out shootings or executions, has launched a petition in which they affirm: 'We will no longer take part in the destruction, assassination, blockading, starvation and humiliation of the entire Palestinian people.' They have no problems with their normal duties but refuse to act as occupiers of Palestinian land.

Somehow managing to resist any attempt to politicise it, this refusal has inspired the youth, the Israeli left and pacifists, who are now taking to the streets of Tel Aviv and Jerusalem demanding an end to war. It was undoubtedly a very brave decision in a country where the army is more than an institution, in the context of a political culture where refusal is equated with treason. As Tanya Reinhart bluntly says it, 'the military is the most stable and the most dangerous political factor in Israel, one that will remain in power long after Sharon falls'.[4]

A petition was launched on January 25, 2002 and has already received 480 signatures. Four of these have already paid for their refusal with a prison sentence.[5] In addition there are about 400 soldiers who have so far quietly refused to cross the Green Line under Sharon's orders prior to the petition, while according to Israeli media, for every soldier who airs his opinions in public there are at least nine more who hold the same view but are too terrified to speak out.

The refusal to serve in the Gaza Strip and the West Bank brought home a new reality to the Israeli people who were constantly told they were in the right. It made them aware that their beloved army is not fighting terror in the Territories; it is creating it.

And it is the veterans who took part in bombardments and mass executions who claim it. That is probably why they cannot be dismissed, why they can be trusted.

At the same time and notwithstanding strong international criticism, Israel's military services are still conducting a systematic campaign of elimination of suspected members of Islamic groups. In this scheme Operation Defensive Shield has dealt a severe blow, at least in the short term, to the armed organizations. In Nablus, Tulkarm and Jenin the two main groups, Hamas and Islamic Jihad, were decapitated of their leaderships.

More then a hundred suspects have been liquidated in the last 19 months, sometimes by car-bombs, sophisticated devices or, more frequently, by Apache helicopter missiles (about 60 bystanders have also been killed in such operations). It is a state-authorised shoot to kill policy on a huge scale.

Most governments which have carried out extra-judicial executions deny them. Israel, instead, has repeatedly stated that eliminating those perceived to be a threat to the state is government policy and is therefore legal.

The Israelis claim 'it is needed to take out of the equation people who may be involved in acts of terrorism and in some cases those who may be involved in terrorism in the future'. But it is still a systematic campaign of extra-judicial assassination. They initially said they would have been carried out 'only if it was necessary to stop a terrorist cell on its way to commit an attack'; then, since July 2001, new guidelines were issued by the Israeli government to allow the killing of 'known terrorists even if they are not going to commit an attack'.

However, by now there seems hardly any limit to who can become the target of assassination, since the Israeli administration regards the whole Palestinian population as 'known terrorists'.

Notes

1. More than 8,000 Palestinians have already been arrested during the operation, the only requirement for deportation being that they are male, Arab and aged between 13 and 80. They have been taken into special custody (those from the armed organizations) or detained in military camps such as Ofra (West Bank) in terrible conditions, beaten, in some cases tortured, refused any legal representation for up to 18 days; many have been dumped miles from home or inside Israeli settlements. According to the Israelis, 6,000 have already been freed but this is still impossible to verify and hardly believable considering that they plan to reopen the Ketsiot prison. Built to house thousands of prisoners during the first Intifada, the camp in the Negev Desert became synonymous with Israeli brutalities and human rights abuses.
2. In actual fact the balance seems to have been considerably higher. Eye witnesses reported the case of 20 soldiers entering a house which was promptly blown up. None of those who entered could possibly have survived. The explosion was seemingly caused by three missiles shot by an Apache helicopter. For two days the neighbours heard moans, groans, shouting and cries for help from beneath the rubble. When tanks bombed the heap of debris no further sounds were heard.
3. The UN Agency for Palestinian Refugees, which has already provided 640 schools and 140 clinics throughout the Occupied Territories.
4. Tanya Reinhart, *Israel/Palestine: How to end the war of 1948*. New York: Seven Stories Press, 2002.
5. Since the beginning of the Intifada at least 114 conscientious objectors have been imprisoned, with about 20 of them serving jail sentences at present.

6.

Hebron

The Israelis usually refer to it as 'self-defence'. The American and European governments call it 'the peace process' On the ground it is simply apartheid and ethnic cleansing.

Actually the euphemisms employed by the Israelis are countless: the land taken from the Palestinians has not been appropriated but was 'abandoned' by them; the present siege of the West Bank cities is merely an 'encirclement'; the deportation of thousands of Palestinians is declared to be a 'transfer'.

At the beginning of the summer 2002, the Palestinian state promised by about eighty UN resolutions and eight peace agreements, has become landless people subjected to military occupation and territorial expropriation. It may be internationally recognized but among the hills of the West Bank, the Palestinian state barely exists other then as a vague memory, as an idea or as a willful statement of the self-determination of the people.

That becomes impressively evident when our journey heads towards the most southern province of the West Bank, a voyage into a past without a future.

There are children growing up between tanks, women searching for food in a pile of rubbish in the wilderness on the outskirts while the city of Hebron, in the deep south of the West Bank, remains hidden between the rolling hills. Angry special forces soldiers prevent anyone from approaching the enclosed military area.

Reaching Hebron, Palestine's most industrialized city, is never easy. Since the start of the Intifada, all access roads to the town have been blocked by mountains of debris, big cement blocks, barbed wire and moats. Only the Israeli army can enter through special gaps.

The city has a unique composition; about 400 Israeli settlers (70 families in all) are concentrated in three settlements in the ancient city of Hebron, protected by some 3,000 soldiers patrolling the city and maintaining a state of terror with their tanks and helicopters over 140,000 Palestinians. This has made the town one of the most bitterly contested issues in both the conflict and its resolution process. The city of Hebron is at the very heart of Israeli history; they repeat that 'if we do not have the right to live here, we do not have the right to live in any other place'.

Despite the promise of gradually reducing the number of settlements without erecting new ones, the Israeli government insists on a highly provocative policy.

Thirty-four new Israeli outposts have already been established in the West Bank. Defended by thousands of soldiers, these townships made of tower blocks, constructed with local pink stone, are usually built on the top of the hills and are surrounded by a few hundred yards of no-go area ploughed by bulldozers.

'Settlements are not obstacles to peace, but rather contribute to peace'; these are Ariel Sharon's words. As Minister of Infrastructure between 1978 and 1981, he established dozens of settlements in the West Bank region of Galilee, believing that they 'give Israel the depth it needs and the water sources and the essential strategic assets between the coastal plain and the Jordan River'.

Today there are 140 Israeli settlements in the West Bank and their presence has badly affected the local economy by making the movement of people and goods too time-consuming or even impossible. Many Palestinian towns are ringed by settlements linked by a protected road network.[1] Obviously the strategy of maintaining and extending the settlements is meant to ensure maximum Israeli territorial expansion.

It is a spider web created by the Labour government, championed by Likud, and executed by the IDF under the cover of the Oslo Agreement (and built with US and European funds) and with the international knowledge that behind each and every settlement, kibbutz, or town, there was an Arab identity.

Paradoxically, Israel started erecting such an apartheid system at the time (May 1994) when apartheid in South Africa (supported only by Israel's premier Golda Meir) was being dismantled.

While Palestinian refugees are denied the 'right to return', every Jew in the world enjoys the right to do so if they wish, being rewarded with more than $20,000 on arrival. Despite massive state subsides and financial incentives from Zionist organizations abroad, few take this offer up and many brand new houses are still unoccupied.

Some settlements, particularly those in exposed areas, are home to just a few dozen people. Some, like those in the Jordan Valley, were erected as a first line of defence against invasion from the east. Some, for instance those in Hebron, were built for religious or historical reasons. Others, like those in the Gaza Strip, are there simply to oppress the Palestinians in every possible way.[2] All of them ignite confrontations and instigate violence.

When the peace talks started in 1991 there were 110,000 Israeli settlers living in the Occupied Territories. At the start of the present Intifada there were 194,000 settlers scattered throughout the West Bank and approximately 200,000 living in East Jerusalem. Palestinians living in the West Bank zone live at a maximum distance of six miles from Israeli controlled areas (army bases and settlements). For political reasons, some settlements may shrivel and die but the largest ones, in Southern Gaza or around Jerusalem, have been built to stay. Today, for the first time ever, many settlers are speaking openly to the Israeli media about their wish to leave, especially those living in exposed or isolated colonies. Not in Hebron, a city which could be compared to the capital of the religious extremist minority, with strong connection with the military establishment.

I think of the settlers' children and of how much violence has been imposed on them. They are brought up between walls and inside a culture of hatred, surrounded by the Arabs and by their own army and obliged to grow up amid historical falsification and religious illusions.

The uprising has witnessed a sharp increase in settler violence against Palestinian lives and property. Here in Hebron the violence and raids of the settlers increase disproportionately during curfew (which applies, obviously, only to the Arabs) and on Saturdays when the Jewish Sabbath ends. Alleyways and courtyards in the Palestinian part of the old city are covered with metal wiring to ward off showers of stones and other objects from the other side of the wall. Some Palestinian families have to live with an IDF sniper perched on their roofs.

Eye witnesses indicate that often the same group of settlers is involved in attacks in Hebron or Nablus or other West Bank urban centres, pointing to some degree of coordination and collusion in the attacks. Mostly such attacks occur in full view of the Israeli army, sometimes even under its protection or with its active participation.

Human rights groups have documented a long list of racist attacks which included maiming, butchering, torture and killing. Issam Hamad's story is an example of the settlers' supremacist attitude and actions. He was coming home to his Um Sufa village when he was kidnapped by a group of Israelis from the Halamish settlement; his face was burned, his hands broken, he had bruises everywhere and was finished off with a blow on the head with a sharp object.[3]

Probably the most notorious of such attacks happened when an American Jew by the name of Baruch Goldstein, a doctor, accompanied by one or two accomplices, walked into the Ibrahimi Mosque in the centre of Hebron. He was a militant of the anti-Arab and racist movement founded by Rabbi Meir Kahane, who was killed in New York in 1990.

This is one of the most contested sites in Hebron and indeed in the whole of Palestine. The Jews call it the Tomb of the Patriarchs, the Muslims the Ibrahimi Mosque. Around this site there is a wall, still partially visible, built by Herod; during the Byzantine era a Christian church was erected on the same land and after the 638 Arab conquest, this same place became a Muslim mosque. In 1500 a small Jewish community took refuge here fleeing from the Holy Inquisition; they lived here until a massacre in 1929 which left 67 people dead. British troops evacuated the remaining population. [4]

The synagogue being beside the mosque, Jewish settlers and Palestinians had to walk the same garden to enter their own place of worship. IDF soldiers still surround the holy site despite the fact that the mosque has since been closed.

It was Friday February 25, 1994, a few weeks after the signing of the Declaration of Principles. At 5.20 in the morning Goldstein, dressed in a military uniform and armed with a Galil sub-machine gun, broke into the mosque and opened fire on kneeling people, killing 29 and injuring over 200. Goldstein was then attacked by worshippers in the mosque. The Israeli army posted outside the mosque did not step in until the first shootings were over. They killed some of those who had attacked Goldstein and pursued some of the wounded to finish them off. Troops outside sealed off the exits and shot those fleeing the mosque; they fired at the ambulances and chased the injured through the doors of the hospital where they proceeded to kill again. Thirty nine more Palestinians were killed by the army in the violence which erupted after the shooting. More death and injury occurred at the funerals, where the mourners were again assaulted. Despite the IDF intervention Goldstein was killed by members of the congregation.

Instead of being regarded as a great embarrassment to his supporters, Goldstein is highly considered and honoured by them to the present day. After his death, his burial place was transformed into a shrine and became a mausoleum to celebrate his life and deeds. Furthermore, a monument has been erected in his honour in the main square of his Hebron settlement. After the IDF dismantled this controversial monument, a group of settlers reciprocated by desecrating the tomb of the nationalist leader Izzedin Al Qassam in Haifa. As a consequence of this action the monument to Goldstein was promptly reconstructed.

The Ibrahimi Mosque massacre marked the beginning of the end of a weeks-old peace process. During the following months Hamas retaliated by starting a new military campaign, blowing up buses using human bombs.

Khaled, a local journalist in Hebron, claims that:

They want more and more land and less and less Arabs. They only wish us to disappear from Israel's space, history and memory. Once they have finished carving up Palestinians into bantustans they will feel more besieged than ever by the new Palestinian cantonisation.

Israel is the only state in the world without a constitution, without borders and a national identity. If the Israeli war machine is intensifying the ferocity of its occupation, it means that Israel feels it is losing. For the racist and exclusivist settlers it is a bitter pill to swallow.

Notes

1. The colonisation of Arab territories by the Jews actually began in 1878 with the Petah Tiqwa settlement, now a district in the suburbs of Tel Aviv.
2. Palestinian areas around the settlement have increasingly become the dumping ground for solid waste from the colonies. Actually, the town of Abu Dis, cynically invoked by the Israelis as a possible capital of a future Palestinian state, has been used as an unsanitary dumping site for refuse from West Jerusalem.
3. During his funeral in Ramallah, the mourners learned of two Israeli soldiers being held in the town's PNA police station. The barracks was attacked and the soldiers were brutally killed. They were believed to be members of an Israeli special unit, called 'Mustaribeen', responsible for the capture and assassination of many Palestinian activists.
4. In 1960, Rabbi Moshe Levinger led a group of Jews dressed as Swiss tourists into Hebron reclaiming a Jewish presence in the area. After years and years of violence, the IDF proceeded to divide and militarise the city.

7.

There are other Jenins

While the world has remained focused on Jenin, the stories unfolding from other Palestinian cities, villages and refugee camps indicate that the IDF has been engaged in human rights violations in the whole of the West Bank.

'Jenin is not so different from any of the other areas attacked; equally serious violations took place elsewhere, particularly in Ramallah and Nablus', confirms Human Rights Watch researcher Peter Bouckart.[1]

Ten miles south of the devastated refugee camp in Jenin and sunk between the mountains, the city of Nablus is counting its deaths. On April 3, at dusk, hundreds of Israeli tanks, armoured vehicles and caterpillars entered the city from the west, south and east. The refugee camps of Balata and Askar, on the outskirts of Nablus and the casbah, bore the blunt of the assault.

Alleged army brutalities and executions had also accompanied the battle for the hive of lanes and stone houses in the old city, right in the heart of Nablus, the second largest city on the West Bank. The casbah and the old city form a small quarter of the modern city lying under Mount Gerizim and dominated by new buildings on the upper slopes which have been turned into Israeli sniper emplacements. The old city dates back to 71 BC and is home to a priceless heritage left by the Romans, the Byzantines, the Arabs and the Ottoman Empire. In its labyrinth of alleyways the houses are of extremely solid, stone construction, and that is why, although the Merkavas and the bulldozers damaged a vast section of the casbah, the scale of the destruction has not reached the levels of that at Jenin.

Its mosque was transformed into a morgue, just like in Jenin, with the bodies of 54 Palestinians. The city at the heart of the Holy Land was rendered an unholy mess by the IDF, with a taste for targeting such sites; three mosques and a Greek Orthodox church were heavily hit by F16 jet fighters and Apache helicopters.

The 220 year-old eastern entrance of the Khan, the old market, was completely destroyed. Sixty houses were pulverised, and more than 200 were partially destroyed. 'Taggart Building', the British Mandate structure which now houses the local authority, was shelled by six tanks.

No final figures on Operation Defensive Shield are available yet,[2] but the picture is taking shape. It is not only the question of the Jenin and Nablus assaults, but also the fact that an entire population is paying a very high price in terms of suffering. They are prevented from leading a normal daily life; even opening a window is to run the risk of getting shot by IDF snipers. Everything is turned into a matter of life and death.[3]

In Nablus the IDF opened fire into crowded markets, mosques, the hospital and demolished every symbol of the Palestinian National Authority. First reports indicate that there may have been more identified Palestinian casualties (80) and fewer Israelis killed (4) than in Jenin. More children, not necessarily throwing stones, have been killed by fragmented bullets, which are banned under the Geneva Convention, while clearly posing no obvious threat to heavily armoured tanks. Seventy-one bodies have already been identified, five of them children.

Children like seven year old Sabra, from the Askar refugee camp just outside Nablus. He was bringing some water to his neighbours through the backyard when a shell fired from a tank parked 200 yards away killed him along with six other people.

Like Ahmad, whose father was ordered out in the street by the army and was murdered at point blank in front of his family for refusing to do so. The soldiers grabbed Ahmad and ordered him out of the house. 'I was just outside the door when I heard the security catch clicking behind me and I ran for cover.' He was hit twice in the back but managed to crawl to safety.[4]

A large family trapped in their house reported the body of a Palestinian fighter lying in the street outside. When their neighbours tried to reach the body, IDF soldiers shot at them. From the window they watched the unknown fighter die; then they watched the dogs eat his body as it decomposed.

What will happen when the children of Jenin or Nablus, now only a few years of age, grow up maimed or as orphans? What will happen in, say, ten years time when this generation is old enough to understand?

South-east of Nablus and along the Jordan Valley, Merkava tanks, camouflaged like tiger sharks, wait for a prey by the side of the road; they are not here to fight another army, just a civilian population.

Dusty villages lie abandoned and empty. Just like in Ireland, a journey through this country, even if short, is not simply moving through space; it is also moving through time. It is breathing history, a history nurtured with blood. The desert spreads through the cone-shaped mountains and the road is hacked from the bowels of the earth; only the Bedouins live in this forsaken landscape on the spine of the Judean highlands.

Deep in the Dead Sea valley, a plume of black smoke rises from the town of Jericho. Clearly visible a few miles in the distance, the oldest city in the world has been spared the force of the latest invasion despite being sealed off for more than two weeks.

But while their army is persecuting and oppressing, Israelis float in the Dead Sea waters and tan in the sunshine with layers of salt crystallizing on their skin, relaxing, trying to have a normal life. But how can life be normal with signs of mayhem on the horizon?

According to the Book of Genesis (19: 24-26), these waters hide the likely site of Sodom and Gomorrah, 'the cities God destroyed for their immorality by raining sulphur and fire from the sky'. The boys singing on the beach, although acting innocently, add insult to injury; involuntarily they provide another perfect photograph of the morality of the Israeli occupation.[5]

Checkpoints around Jericho, checkpoints on the road to Hebron and along the motorway to Jerusalem. The closure of the Occupied Territories is nothing new to the conflict and has little to do with Operation Defensive Shield. Checkpoints along the Green Line and around Gaza were set up after Oslo but since the start of the Intifada the siege have become permanent; and that is why these road blocks are now one of the most distinguishing and hated features of the Palestinian uprising.

No one is allowed through them, even the terminally ill or the pregnant. There have been hundreds cases where people were due their chemotherapy or dialysis treatment but the IDF refused to let them out; many of them, according to the International Red Cross, have since died. In December 2001 two young mothers were held at the Salem/Jenin checkpoint and their infants, only a few days old, subsequently died in the village because of the delay in getting proper care.

After 19 months of conflict, curfews and invasions have sadly become the routine rather than the exception. Like incursions or air raids, these military aggressions, apparently motivated only by revenge, mark weakness not strength.

The Qalandia checkpoint, just outside Ramallah, is jammed with traffic. Merchants have set out their stalls along the muddy road, selling everything from hummus to camels. On the side of the road there is a line of empty trucks, used to carry people to work in Israel, which have been 'decommissioned' by IDF soldiers. A long queue of women with infants, schoolchildren and elderly people waits in the pouring rain.

The city, half a mile away, is into the third week of military curfew and no one can get in or out. A dusty footpath around the adjoining hills is the only possible route; it is a veritable sniper's alley, 200 yards within the firing range of both Israeli soldiers and settlers, with no rocks or trees for cover.

Since the start of the latest assault the city has been heavily bombarded, with tanks, artillery and helicopters firing into schools, shopping centres, mosques and every PNA installation or building.

Around Manara Square the curfew has just been lifted for two hours and people rush out in the streets only to find a few empty shops open. They may be murdered at any minute because the snipers are firing even during the short ceasefire, tossing stun grenades from time to time.

'Malnutrition is spreading', says Dr Atari in the city hospital, 'causing an increased number of deaths among children and old people'.

> Many people are dying every day in the West Bank, not just the wounded left bleeding to death by the IDF, but all those stopped at checkpoints and prevented from getting treatment, all those who get ill because the humanitarian convoys are stopped at Qalandia.

People here had suffered the economic embargo symbolized by the IDF checkpoints for 17 months before Operation Defensive Shield was launched. In the last two years throughout Palestine, Israeli troops have uprooted centuries-old plantations, destroyed harvests, incinerated crops, razed local factories to the ground, shelled infrastructures and, of course, erected new settlements. The whole of Palestine is only over 400 kilometres long from north to south, but because of the Israeli settlers and soldiers even a ten minute journey may take hours.

Since the Oslo Agreement Israel has effectively incorporated the Palestinian economy, keeping it in a permanent state of dependency. Because of the hermetic closure of the checkpoints, today a little under a million Palestinians depend on the International Red Cross for their subsistence and food. In the wake of Defensive Shield, the Palestinian economy, even if the siege were lifted now and the Intifada ceased instantly, would take years to recover.

Beside the hospital there is an empty car park in the shade of pine trees. The wind blows sand and dust from a bank of soil towards the edge of the parking lot. This is a mass grave. Twenty-seven men and two women were buried here ten days ago because the hospital had run out of space for dead bodies. Eighty-one Palestinians have already been killed in Ramallah since early April but many more remain unaccounted for.

On the opposite side of the hill stands Yasser Arafat's compound, the 'Muqata'. Since December 2001 Abu Ammar[6] has been placed under virtual house arrest by Sharon's army. The Israeli premier accuses him of not doing enough to stop the suicide bombers and of tacitly supporting their actions while publicly condemning them. As a matter of fact, in his failed attempt to delegitimize his life-long enemy, Sharon is only delegitimizing himself and emphasising the brutality of the military occupation.

A mother with three small children is determined to show me the destruction caused to her home. Only the kitchen and the living room are still standing in this house which faces the Muqata. The family is smoking from narghilee and drinking coffee while watching the Merkavas patrolling Arafat's headquarters. They simply sit there on the sofa, observing and commenting on the manoeuvre as if following a football match on television. 'It is not bad for a peace process. This is the peace we have won. Instead of Palestinian independence we have won Palestinian dependence on Israel. Instead of having a peace settlement, we have Jewish settlements', they joke.

All around Arafat's headquarters the muddy road is littered with empty cases of rubber and live bullets; Israeli Special Forces have commandeered all the upper storeys in the surrounding buildings without even bothering to conceal cannons and machine guns. The tanks' engines may be switched off but the turrets follow everyone's movements, accompanied by a chilly, electric lament.

Ramallah: a Merkava 3 tank patrols the district around Yasser Arafat's compound in April 2002.

In a small building within the compound, five unarmed PNA policemen were executed, significantly, beside the sign of the Centre for the Diffusion of Democracy, only last week. All the armed personnel in the compound, excluding 40 people still living with Arafat, have been killed during IDF attacks – that means dozens of deaths.

The compound was once a hastily built, incomplete palace, like most buildings in the rest of Palestine. Now the IDF has demolished the outer walls and the barracks, leaving only two small buildings standing; they are now literally only one wall away from the Palestinian president. But obviously it is not just the life and career of the old lion that is at stake here; it is the struggle for freedom and self-determination of an entire people.

This leaves the Israeli authorities caught in the contradiction of destroying every installation of the very PNA police whom they say should arrest the militants. Sharon asks the impossible from Arafat; he wants the dispersed PNA leadership to achieve the capture of all those he considers 'terrorists', something that not even the most sophisticated intelligence service in the world, the Israeli one, has been capable of achieving in 54 years.

The Palestinian leadership appears totally besieged and not only by the tanks and helicopter gun-ships. The threat comes also from within. The international community has asked him to reform the Authority and he has called for new elections, which he had postponed in 1999, to be held in February 2003.

Internal opposition appears even harder to cope with after 17 people were killed in a car bombing, claimed by the Islamic Jihad[7] at the Megiddo Junction, a few miles from Jenin, in early June. CIA chief George Tenet delivered a simple message to Arafat: if there is another Megiddo the US can no longer guarantee his safety (while before the episode the Bush administration had guaranteed that 'he wouldn't be harmed'). A plan to shift the PNA leadership to Gaza had been agreed between Tel Aviv and Washington last winter.

It is a highly risky game; the Jihad and Hamas movements are backed by over one third of the Palestinian population and Arafat's death would prove to the hard-liners that no peace is possible as long as Israel still exists.

So the Muqata is now the place where a deliberate or accidental bullet might well turn the tide of history in the Middle East. The life of the Palestinian President still hangs by a thread. A living Arafat may talk of peace; a dead one will catapult the Middle East into a far broader and bloodier conflict.

Notes

1. Source: *Ha'Aretz*, 22.4.2002
2. According to B'Tselem and other Israeli human rights organizations, Operation Defensive Shield registered an average of 65 people killed each day during the first two weeks of the attack.
3. The occupation is still ongoing in dozens of towns and bloody incursions, like in Qalqilya, are still causing deaths and injuries. Israeli flags are still waving in Dura and in the small villages like Shuweiki, Balah and Shufi. Most of these villages are situated within the ten kilometre exclusion zone proposed by Sharon last February and after months of military curfew, there may be worse to come.
4. Source: B'Tselem.
5. It is worth remembering that not every Israeli supports his/her government's actions in the Territories. There are a few pacifists and left-wing groups opposing the regime, generally harassed by the state and censored by the media. Over the last few weeks they have staged impressive protests at checkpoints; they were welcomed in Ramallah by President Arafat before getting assaulted by their own army outside the compound. In another protest they sneaked through the military lines and into the West Bank's hospitals with medical supplies and blood bags for those, Palestinians as well as Israelis, injured at the height of the March violence. Many intellectuals, not only Israelis, including Nobel Peace Prize winners, have described Israeli behaviour in the Territories as 'worse than the Nazis'.
6. Arafat's 'nomme de guerre'.
7. The smaller of the two Islamic armed groups, it developed in the Gaza Strip in the early 1970s. Its leader, Fathi Shaqaqi, was assassinated by an Israeli hit squad in Malta in 1995.

8.

From the Church of the Nativity

'This was the road Joseph and Mary walked to get to the spot where Jesus was born. Today they would probably be shot like anyone else, pregnant or not', said Mr. Sansur, who lives in an old house on the road to Bethlehem. The street has been renamed after Yasser Arafat and the road sign, riddled with bullet holes, has been knocked down by IDF tanks.

The house stands right on the interface between Aida refugee camp on the outskirts of Bethlehem and Israeli army positions. Inside, within a frame on the wall, Mr. Sansur has collected all his family's keys. When they were deported after Israel's birth in 1948, Palestinian refugees took with them the keys of the houses they lived in, hoping to return one day.

Mr. Sansur's house overlooks the refugee camp, built around a mosque and a school on the rolling slopes of the hill. On the opposite hill Israelis had placed tanks and concealed artillery. The size of the Gilo settlement on the hills above adds to the sense of fear.

In the labyrinth of muddy, narrow alleyways and unfinished white houses scarred by missiles and shells, the Aida refugee camp could be compared to a ghetto – no services, no facilities, no amenities, nothing. There are neither shops nor playing fields, only ruins and anguish.

The echoes of children crying, wailing sirens, electric wires dangling from folded pylons. Conditions are worse than inhumane; thousands of people, mostly children, breathe misery and endemic poverty. Kids show their bullet wounds, old men drag their sorrow through debris and rubbish.

In Aida Palestinians are harassed even after death; there used to be a cemetery at the bottom of the hill, but the IDF desecrated it with their bulldozers.

Ibraimh, once a teacher in the local school, told me:

> We live in a laager; this is an open prison and they put us down like animals. That's what we are for them, animals. We have nothing; these children have nothing. We have no rights and nothing to defend us or fight back, only our songs and our culture.

The derelict two storey building, funded by UN aid, was draped with blue flags and red crosses but the international display did not spare the school from being bombarded and fired upon while pupils were still inside it.

Within the building there was a gallery of horrors. The windows of the classrooms facing IDF positions have been bricked up and a line of sandbags borders the wall; on the floor piles of burnt-out schoolbooks stood as a monument to human cruelty. A dense trail of machine-gun holes was scattered along halls and corridors.

'My teddy bear is afraid; I'm not', whispers a four year old child holding Ibraimh's hand tightly. The schoolchildren's drawings sent a chill up and down my spine; they feature helicopters like giant spiders raining missiles on a slide, fire, flames and bloodstains, dead children and crying parents, tanks like dragons spitting flames on their houses and school.

Some of the children had been separated from their families, some were orphans; they had very few dreams and even less future. They did not hate the 'bad boys' for shelling them; they simply could not understand why. They lined up to shake hands in the yard, with their deep, dark eyes ransacking the conscience, their whole life concentrated in their laughter. One little girl was sobbing in a corner. I had nothing to console her, so I gave her the only thing I had: a flower. She cupped it lovingly in the palms of her hands, smiled through her sunny tears and ran towards the teacher, followed by her friends. 'Everyone is asking for a petal', translated Ibraimh.

It cannot be easy to drop your children to school knowing that 'Zionist' artillery may wipe them out with one single shell. Apart from the Holy Cross school in the Ardoyne area of North Belfast, there are few other places in the world where this would be allowed to happen. 'Schools have become frequent and easy targets for Apache missiles throughout Palestine and with 60 percent of our population under the age of 18, there will be more innocent deaths', cautioned the teacher.

A refugee himself, Salah was working hard to set up a community centre for children, a few yards from the school, 'only to give them some distraction, sometimes a roof or just a place to stay away from the bullets.'

The doors of the centre have been used as a mural; a long key is shaped to form the date 1948. Beyond the coloured doors the place is desolately empty. Of course Salah has huge obstacles to surmount.

> We have nothing here, two rooms and one computer; we're doing a programme of local activities for a hundred children. It is everyone's duty to try to build something for their tomorrow. Their today is in the tanks on the opposite hill. And that's what they play with most of the times.

To emphasise the point, he showed me an unexploded helicopter missile warhead.

Since then I have spoken on the phone to Salah a few times over the last three months before losing all contact with him. A new IDF assault of the refugee camp in March 2002 had convinced the male population to leave the area in order to avoid mass arrests.

When the Israelis arrived they found only women, children and elderly people. After the IDF had left, Salah returned to 'his' kids in Aida; that was only a few days before Sharon's Defensive Shield operation.

When I returned in mid-April, at the height of the Operation, Bethlehem was a ghost town. Less than three weeks into the new assault this is still strictly a military zone and death is the only presence here.

A classroom line of defence into the Aida refugee camp primary school. The Israeli tanks are a hundred yards distant from the sand-bagged wall.

The town cannot even bury its own dead; bodies are still lying in the streets which are littered with rubbish and debris. Nuns have been shot at, priests murdered, paramedics fired on indiscriminately, churches and schools bombed; even the white statue of the Virgin Mary on top of its pillar in the city centre was sprayed and blackened by machine-gun fire for being a prominent terrorist infrastructure. Yet the suffering of the people living in Jesus' hometown hardly stirs up any reaction in the Vatican, apart from its usual general and empty appeals for calm and restraint.

Guided by a Palestinian stringer and advancing with our hands in the air, dreading the IDF snipers, we try to reach Bethlehem city centre when two army personnel carriers surround us and, pointing their machine-guns, order us to leave immediately. After the first warning a bullet usually follows, rarely shot in the air. So a few minutes later, on hearing the tanks coming back, we run for shelter, stopping only to ring a front-door bell on the way. Without asking any question they open the gate just a few seconds before the armoured patrol returns.

We find ourselves inside a French convent. Even its gardens bear the scars of Israeli contempt for basic human rights. An old gardener is the only presence around. Inside the main building, on the first floor, Sister Munira unveils an unbelievable island of tenderness in this ocean of hate.

It is hard to hold back tears. Yet, maybe not even tears suffice to describe what we actually witness. With two other nuns, Munira runs an orphanage housing about 45 children. The oldest ones, four or five years old, run to us for a hug.

Few of the children here were abandoned; eight of them had both their parents killed in the Intifada; in two cases they are the only survivors of entire families wiped out by the Israelis. Nine infants are in their cots next door; a tiny girl is enjoying her very first smiles but there is no one there to record them.

In the last weeks the nuns bravely challenged the curfew, searching the town for milk and bread to feed the children. 'The army broke in, terrorising the children and scaring them out of their wits', accuses sister Munira. 'The oldest children went hysterical, crying and screaming for days. They couldn't sleep and they wet their beds. Soldiers shouted in their ears that they were going to bomb the whole place. Is this human?'

In the Beit Jala hospital, just across the road from the convent, the latest body has just arrived. 'The IDF confiscated Atallah's house; he refused to leave so they put him in the car and told him to drive away, to be shot by the snipers', says Dr Kumri. 'Atallah was 82 years of age and was killed by a high-velocity bullet which entered the back of his head'.

On the first floor those wounded during the IDF invasion are packed into small rooms. I inquire to see if Salah is in any of the hospital wings, or if his name is contained in any of the death bulletins. A paramedic informs me.

After April 2, when the IDF attacked Bethlehem, Salah survived the heavy shelling and found shelter inside the Church of the Nativity. Similarly to what happened in Jenin, political and armed militants from all factions buried their differences and defended the city alongside PNA security forces. When the tanks rolled into Bethlehem the combatants and those passing near the Church of the Nativity had no choice but to seek refuge within the 1,400 year-old building.

Speaking on the mobile phone on April 19, Salah tells me:

> There's about 200 of us. There are also about 30 Franciscan monks and some families with children. The Israelis have burst the water pipes and drained the wells. We had shared the poor food the monks had in the convent and until a few days ago we ate half a cup of rice each. Now it's been more than a week without any food at all, for all of us. The IDF don't allow any food or medical supplies but we are fine; our spirits are high. We know that in three or four days' time maybe we will start to die, one by one. And the army outside knows that too. Yet they still attack us with grenades, machine guns and snipers, even if time is on their side.

A huge army crane has been placed in Manger Square, just outside the church; it holds loudspeakers bombarding the town with noises from horror films: scratching sounds, women screaming, dogs barking. Sometimes the many other churches in Bethlehem ring their own bells to cover the white noise.

'Sharon offered us the choice between permanent exile and prosecution by an Israeli court', explains Salah. 'He asked us to surrender in two different ways. But we will not. The man can transfer us to another country but some of us will come back. He can kill us within these ancient walls but someone else will take our place in the next church.'

> And anyway, we are lucky to be still here, I mean alive, when so many of our children and women and comrades are being killed in Palestine every day. I don't feel full of sorrow because I'm here and the Israelis are firing at us; but you know how many friends I had in Jericho, Gaza, Jenin, Ramallah and I can't find anyone. They are all dead. My brothers are dead; my country is dying.

Salah's voice weakens.

> We don't know how many Jenins Sharon is prepared to plunder to see all of us out of our land once and for all. We are all his hostages; the Middle East is his hostage; the UN and the European Community are his hostages; even the American administration is his hostage. This man can act above any law and kill as much as he wishes.

Towards the end of April, in the holiest of Christian places, where Jesus is believed to have been born, more than 200 people may be about to die either by a bullet or through starvation. The Israelis besiege and assault the holy site, while blaming the Palestinians for having violated it.

Eight Palestinians are murdered by IDF snipers while trying to collect grass from the convent garden because there is nothing left to eat. Two of them, wounded in the shooting, bleed to death while trying to crawl to their comrades. The church's bell-ringer is killed by the IDF; three monks, a nun and 14 other people are injured but the Israelis refuse to let in any medical supply.

Conditions inside the small church are rapidly deteriorating; there's one toilet for more than 200 people and there is no water. The children are becoming ill; a Palestinian has an Israeli bullet stuck in his leg; some are losing their sight while many have lost up to 20 kilograms in weight; others are coughing or vomiting blood. Some of the monks, in the Orthodox quadrant of the convent, refuse to share their food supplies while the weakest among the Palestinians are starving to death.

During the talks aimed at ending the deadlock, the Israelis obtained a list of everyone inside. Their houses will then be bombed, shelled with helicopter missiles or raided.

On May 2, after three vain attempts to solve the impasse, the Israelis seem to be about to end the stand-off by storming into the church, but the action of a group of ten pacifists prevents a bloodbath. Carrying rice, fruit, cigarettes and medicines, they reach the small Door of Humility and slip into the church. Now forced to take action, the Vatican, the European Union and the US launch a diplomatic mediation which will finally end the siege on Friday May 10.[1]

After six long weeks Salah leaves the church in the morning rain; separated from his 'brothers' and dearest friends he is allowed to return home. At the very end, when it seemed that the church was going to become their grave, Salah, his comrades, the religious and the civilians, including the pacifists, have broken the Israeli siege.

As the script is completed the Aida refugee camp, with its school and community centre, will be included in the exclusion zone (works are already underway), planned by Sharon. The children's future like their present and their past, is hovering between death and deportation.

Notes

1. Thirteen Hamas, Jihad and al-Aqsa Brigade militants, all on the
    Israeli wanted list, were taken to Cyprus and from there to different
    European states; 26 Palestinians were exiled to Gaza and all the rest
    were allowed to go home.

9.

The lessons of Sabra and Chatila

Eight years old Jihad cannot savour the breathtaking beauties around him. His father Isa, a refugee from the Hebron ghetto, jokes that 'he might be lucky because he can't see the horrors'.

Like his two older brothers Jihad was born with a genetic disorder which made him blind. But while ten year-old Mohamed is a talented keyboard musician and Abdel walks every day with his stick to the mosque, praying for a miracle, the youngest child's right eye catches glimpses of lights and colour; the family cannot afford to travel to Moscow for the surgical operation that could give him his sight.

Jihad lives in a stone house in Hizma, a small refugee camp between Jerusalem and Ramallah, buried in squalor and despair. The old grandfather in his red kafhia and 14 other people dwell in two empty rooms, sleeping on the floor.

Steam from cups of coffee and tea mixes in the air with smoke clouds from the men's chain-smoking. Isa knows the soldiers are coming.

> They want to build a wall to divide Jerusalem and segregate it from the surrounding Palestinian villages like Hizma. They deported me from my house in Hebron. Now we are going to stay here. It's not simply our houses; to us it is our land; it's our country. In the end, the Jews will fade away exactly like the Romans, the Turks and the British have done.

We just managed to access the camp and unload sacks of rice, vegetables and fruit beside Isa's house before the IDF sealed the entrances off. Jihad writes something in English for me, typing on his Braille machine. In the hurried moments before the curfew the page with colourless words slips from my pocket; Jihad wrote that he dreams of playing the guitar.

IDF soldiers take position along the dusty road. Jihad does not want us to go. My friend, stringer and interpreter Mustapha breaks the agonizing farewell when he hears the tanks approaching from the distance. In a way Jihad epitomises all the staggering encounters, with people you may not see again. Across the whole length of the Territories, from Gaza to Jenin, this is a land of farewells.

Sorrow grows more intense with the realisation that millions of Palestinian refugees and their descendants are still enduring these conditions. To date, they constitute the largest – 3.7 millions displaced – and longest-lasting refugee population in the world.[1] For the Israelis, on the other hand, the camps remain both a political embarrassment and a security nightmare while Sharon, far from conceding their right to return, is creating new refugees on a daily basis.

'Israel must recognize the right of the refugees to return to their homes, to give them the chance to come back. Keeping such a large population without connection to peace will only contribute to the perpetuation of injustice and of the conflict itself', remarks Dr Hanan Ashrawi, spokesperson for the Palestinian delegation at the Madrid 1991 peace talks.

The Israelis claim that the 'right to return' will amount to the end of the Jewish state. But as a matter of fact, today 78 percent of the Israeli population lives in an area equal to only 15 percent of the entire national territory and most of the remaining Israelis live in about 30 urban centres. That leaves less than 200,000 Israelis in control of a huge and largely uninhabited area (expropriated after 1948). If the refugees from Lebanon were permitted to return to Galilee and those living in Gaza were settled in the southern regions where most of them came from, it would barely change the demographic situation of the Israeli majority in the areas they inhabit.

In the words of the Palestinian leader:

> The first and most important step to deal with the refugees question is for Israel to admit its own historical responsibility for their claim and start facing the consequences of such responsibility. We are not asking for the whole of Palestine; we want our state back, within the territories of the pre-1967 Israeli invasion, and the right to be treated as humans, free from this brutal military repression.

Regarded as one of the finest political intellectuals, Dr Ashrawi is among those Palestinian leaders who supports a return to the negotiating table.

> But how could you possibly negotiate with anyone who is sending his tanks and aircraft to kill a defenceless civilian population, children and innocent people? It's shameful. It's cold-blooded aggression, which is in itself part of a wider plan. Bombings and killing of a civilian population prepare the ground for a reoccupation of the Gaza Strip and the West Bank. They're not simply a violation of every international principle and of the peace agreements. They are a violation of human dignity.
>
> The aggression must be brought to an end and a new political avenue should be opened. But it could all be useless because Sharon doesn't want peace; he doesn't need it. What he needs is a military victory to prove to the world that he has eradicated the revolt of those whom in reality he is oppressing with cruelty. But apart from the military occupation and settlements issues, a real and durable conflict resolution won't be possible if the refugees' question isn't properly addressed and Sharon's way to address it is widely known.

On the evening of September 14, 1982, as Minister of Defence, Sharon allegedly attended a meeting with the commanders of the

Lebanese Christian Falangist Militia. At dawn the Israeli army stormed West Beirut and cordoned off all the refugee camps which housed thousands of Palestinians – civilians, as the OLP had just fled to Tunis. The raid began before sunset the following day, the 16th, and continued for more than 36 hours.

Israel had provided its proxy Lebanese militia with maps and pictures and fired flares to turn night into day so that no Palestinians would be able to escape. Those who did flee, mostly women and children, were brought back inside by IDF soldiers to face their destiny.

And their destiny was death. On September 18 the massacre at the Sabra and Chatila camps had reached its peak. No one knows the exact figure but the number of those who were slaughtered is at least 1,500 (800 according to the Israelis, 2,750 according to the international Commission of Inquiry headed by the late Sean Mac Bride). Children were tortured and machetes were used to cut them into pieces; women were raped and butchered. According to witness reports there was a special torturing squad which specialized in cracking skulls, disembowelling pregnant women, mutilating limbs and trailing victims around the camp until the final blow.

'They came from the mountains in 30 huge trucks', recalls Hasan, one of the survivors, in Amnoun Kabliyouk's book *Sabra and Chatila: The Investigation of a Massacre.*

> At first they started killing people with knives so that they wouldn't make any noise. Then they put snipers in the Chatila camp to kill anybody who crossed the street. Next, armed men began going into the houses killing men, women and children. At the end they blew up the houses, sometimes with people in them, burying bodies under piles of rubble.

The Knesset was forced to take action and set up a committee to scrutinise Sharon's involvement in the atrocity. He was found responsible for the actions of the Lebanese Falangists and consequently forced to resign from his post, but he was never charged and never appeared in any court of justice. The Israeli supreme court declared him unfit to command the army, yet he is deemed fit to lead the Israeli government.

Last Christmas Eve, 2001, former Mossad agent, former Lebanese Minister and Syrian spy, Elie Hobelka, was killed in a car-bomb explosion in Beirut. Known to the Palestinians as the Sabra and Chatila executioner, Hobelka had promised to testify before an international human rights tribunal based in Belgium, explaining how the Lebanese Militia was only an instrument in the Israeli Army's arsenal, led by the then Minister of Defence, Ariel Sharon.

While there is very little doubt Hobelka had plenty of enemies in the region, the now Israeli prime minister is the one who mostly benefits from his death. For the families of 23 survivors who brought the case before the court, it is a heavy blow, but their struggle will not be deterred. The accusations are ignominious for Sharon; he may face charges of war crimes and crimes against humanity. A decision was due early in March but was postponed until June 26. At that point the case collapsed because of the death of Hobelka, the chief witness. The Belgian human rights group and the relatives are still hopeful that a case can be taken against Sharon.

No one has ever been charged with responsibility for the massacre. Furthermore the victims have not been properly buried to date; they lie in communal graves, the largest of which are now used as a rubbish dumping ground or the foundations of a recently rebuilt stadium.

Almost exactly 20 years later the Israelis made sure not to repeat the mistakes of Sabra and Chatila, when for days after the slaughter hundreds of bodies were there to be seen and filmed. In Jenin it took the IDF nine days to remove the evidence.

Perhaps the numbers this time did not reach the proportion of the Sabra and Chatila massacres but the similarities between the two are incontestably obvious to everyone. An umbilical cord makes them twin off-spring of the same monster. They were scrupulously planned, ruthlessly executed and viciously covered up.

By now not just the Palestinians but also the bulk of the international humanitarian organizations are denouncing executions and war crimes. Speaking on Israeli radio, Terje Larsen, the UN special envoy for the Middle East, described the refugee camp as 'an inferno and to say it was a massacre it is not exaggerating. This is a repugnant page in Israel's history'.[2] The UN also spoke of 'a war crime on the scale of the Bosnia and Kosovo wars.'

During the attack on Jenin, PNA Minister for Information Abed Rabbo wrote a letter to international bodies and sovereign states denouncing the removal of the bodies of 500 people allegedly killed by the IDF. He was referring only to the armed militants and did not provide any estimate for civilian casualties.

An independent Human Rights Watch report released in May corroborates the accusations of war crimes and confirms 'a provisional number' of 55 deaths nearly equally shared between militants and civilians'.[3] B'Tselem and other peace movements fear the number could be much higher.

In the aftermath of Operation Defensive Shield the Palestinians are struggling with the most basic question of survival. The West Bank is in ruin, public buildings, records and resources have been destroyed by the IDF, thousands of people who fled their cities under attack are now scattered between the surrounding mountains and villages. Obviously, the Palestinian authorities are not able to establish the actual death toll of all those who died in Jenin.

The UNRWA on the other hand, does not have the personnel required to trace all those who lived in the camp before the 2nd of April, when the rape of Jenin began. To conduct such a massive investigation, it would require going over lists of those killed, missing and imprisoned and try to locate them, which is virtually impossible in the present conditions of military occupation.

A new significant clue came unexpectedly on April 29 when IDF General Giora Eiland exposed the first preliminary results of the army internal inquiry on the events in Jenin. He described

the lack of coordination between the different infantry units
on the ground and the incapacity of some IDF officers to

properly interpret information related by the security services; the lack of accurate and detailed information on the exact dislocation of enemy forces; the difficulties for the helicopters to correctly identify and hit the targets.

With sadness, I read of an IDF officer who admitted to Tel Aviv's daily paper *Ma'ariv* having 'tried to adopt the same techniques used by the Germans in the Warsaw ghetto'.

It may be that we will never know the exact number of all of those who died in Jenin. But it is apparent that a Palestinian life is worth less than an Israelian one. The truth remains buried under tons and tons of rubble because Sharon still refuses to allow the UN or international aid into the ruins of the camp.

This suggests that the Israeli government is not so sure after all of being capable of proving its version of events.

In the controversy surrounding claims and counter-claims, scores of refugees who lived in the camp before April 2 are still missing. Behind numbers and figures there are human tragedies: the death of innocent civilians, poor people, ordinary mothers and fathers, small children who have no right to live.

Hopefully, the long search for truth and justice should start from the fact that so much violence was deliberately and sadistically planned well in advance, as every politician or news agency in the world was aware of Sharon's plan for genocide.

His main target was not Palestinian terrorism and its infrastructures; it wasn't simply a question of security. On the contrary, it looks very much like Sharon is effectively trying to dispose of every symbol of Palestinian authority. Bombing offices, schools, hospitals, courts and prisons, he is killing not the terrorists but the negotiators and their credibility. Many believe his ultimate goal is no less than the complete dissolution of the Palestinian national movement.

The state of Israel has not only the right but also an obligation to protect the lives of its citizens, but the measures should be in accordance with international humanitarian law. Human rights abuses by armed groups can never justify violations of fundamental human rights by governments and will not bring security about. Operation Defensive Shield was not about security. Rather it was about control and the destruction of the very fabric of the Palestinian society to the suppression of which the Israeli state owes its 'independence'.

Notes

1. The refugees in Lebanon are under permanent threat from Israeli raids and artillery. In 1996 three 155 mm shells landed on a United Nations base in Qana, packed with 500 people; over 120 refugees were killed. The IDF claimed it was a mistake and no one was prosecuted. The 400,000 Palestinian refugees in Lebanon are banned from nearly 80 professions outside their camps. They cannot teach in Lebanese schools and their children cannot attend them. They cannot be doctors or patients in Lebanon; they cannot own property. Since they cannot leave their camps they are excluded from every aspect of Lebanese society. A very similar situation applies also for Palestinian refugees still confined in Syria (460,000) and Jordan (more than a million). In the PNA-controlled territories there are over 1,400,000 refugees (600,000 in the West Bank alone).

2. Larsen also gave the first figures, noting that 75 percent of local production activities have stopped and unemployment is reaching unprecedented heights. Sharon's invasion has so far cost $450 million but the data are still incomplete because we do not yet know the full scale of the destruction in Jenin and Nablus. The IDF, in four weeks, actually destroyed the vast majority of the infrastructure built by the Palestinians in nine years.

3. According to the US-based organization, 4,000 have been left homeless, 1,350 families have lost everything and 880 houses have been either destroyed or damaged to the extent that they will have to be demolished. At least 700 of the camp's residents have been arrested and are still imprisoned.

10.

Al-Quds/Yerushalayim

Back from the horrors of the West Bank, I returned to Jerusalem to pause. But there is nowhere to hide. The scene is rather controversial; draped with Stars of David and Israeli flags, between parades, firework and street parties, the city is celebrating the 54th anniversary of the Jewish state. Unsurprisingly the Palestinians call it the 'Nakba', the catastrophe. While they have every right to have their own state and to defend themselves, the Israelis shouldn't be allowed to deny statehood to anyone else, let alone in such a violent manner.

At the same time, in the Arab part of the city (most of present-day 'Israeli West Jerusalem' before 1948 had, in reality, a large Palestinian population which was chased from what today is called the 'New City') less than a mile away from the proud celebrations, the IDF are invading two Palestinian districts in East Jerusalem, evicting families to make room for more settlers. No fireworks here, only machine-gun fire.

The city might be under military control but the streets are most definitively taxi-drivers' territory. They dictate the rules by continually beeping the horns. Most of the taxis are equipped with automatic gear-boxes so the drivers can speak interminably on the mobile phone. The taxis are called 'sherutz' and are usually Mercedes or minivans, carrying six to eight people and working on the line of the West Belfast Black Taxis along fixed routes.

Boarding them can be a life-challenge. From Ben Gurion Airport to Jerusalem is only 50 kilometres, but in the morning rush hour it is an hour and a half journey. Smoking and cursing, the taxi driver travelled for 30 kilometres on the hard shoulder, constantly hooting the horn and narrowly missing those trying to pull right. When he finds a jeep blocking his way the driver becomes irritated and after five minutes, he gets out of the van, abandoning his passengers in fear; nearly every Israeli carries a legal weapon. Once he has found a way into Jerusalem we finally think it is all over when an old Orthodox Jew, on the pedestrian crossing, waves his arm announcing he is about to cross the road. Our driver mumbles something and leaning his head toward the steering wheel, he pushes his foot heavily on the accelerator and narrowly misses the old man by inches.

Conquered some 37 times from its foundation and its illegal occupation by Israel in 1967, sacred to three religions, Jerusalem is a city which widely arouses passionate emotions. As far as the Israeli-Palestine question is concerned this city lies at the very heart of the matter, claimed by both sides as their capital.

It was proclaimed an international 'open city' for all religions by the United Nations in 1948 and later invaded by the Israelis on the third morning of the Six Day War. Today the city embraces different political, ethnic and religious components, which have settled here, sometimes contradicting each other, through the centuries.

Israel declared it the single indivisible capital of the Jewish state but not a single foreign state recognizes the city as such. In fact, all the foreign embassies remained in Tel Aviv even after the Knesset had been relocated to Jerusalem.[1] The Israeli government has since challenged countless United Nations resolutions against the measures adopted in Jerusalem.

Al-Quds for the Palestinians, Yerushalayim for the Israelis; two cities, two worlds in one, first class citizens alongside slaves; some have everything, others have nothing. Yet for the Israelis, in the western part of the city, this is all the result of Arab terrorism.

In his manifesto Sharon had pledged to bring peace and security to the region. No Israeli I spoke to seriously believed that electing Sharon would have brought peace but at least they believed he would have delivered security.

This Intifada has almost doubled the number of the Israelis who have died (256) during the post-1985 invasion of Lebanon which was regarded here as a national disaster. The Hizbullah war lasted fifteen years and the vast majority of Israeli casualties were military personnel. This uprising has lasted 19 months and the death toll includes already more than 300 civilians.

To be honest, the Israelis look anything but secure; they usually avoid crowded gatherings for fear of suicide attacks; they appear suspicious and even hostile. They check faces of those entering the restaurants they are eating in or the bus they are travelling on. They look fragile, emotionally scarred and obsessed with history. And the paradox of course is that every Israeli is well aware that, at the end of the day, only the birth of a Palestinian state has the power to bestow full legitimacy on Israel, as well as to ensure 'security' that continuous wars of aggression have never been able to guarantee. Many Israelis have developed a strong feeling of sectarian hatred which will deny a real chance of any political change in the near future.

For more than half a century the Israelis have wanted to pretend that the Palestinian community was not really there. They forced them to forget their past even if the mission of Israel has been to teach the world remembrance, transforming the Palestinians into the victims of the victims, the refugees of the refugees.

It is a highly militarised society, floundering in its Orthodox biblical immobility. The persecution complex of an ever-menaced people, where the supreme court approves the systematic torture on Palestinian detainees, has made the oppressed oppressors.

From a purely logistical angle, Jerusalem appears paralysed by the crumbling agreements and crushed by the Israeli demand to claim everything for itself.

The phased handover agreed by Israel and only partially implemented, well behind schedule,[2] has mutilated Jerusalem and cut it off from its natural hinterland. All around the city there is a messy patchwork of different areas of control: Area A (6 percent of the Territories) is supposed to be totally under PNA jurisdiction; Area B comprises a large number of Palestinian villages under PNA administration and Israeli security; Area C, including the settlements and the roads linking them, has been placed entirely under Tel Aviv.[3]

However, the centre of contention in Jerusalem is probably the Old City and its surroundings where 28,000 Palestinians and 2,000 Israelis live side by side, a few yards from each other.

Close to the Jaffa Gate, the dome of a mosque reaches up into the starry night. It was once a sacred shrine for Muslims, but the Israelis have turned it into the museum of the Patriarch David. Following the outer wall one arrives at the Zion Gate, a place which the Jews cherish dearly. The ancient walls still bear the pockmarks of bullets of various calibre. It was here the Israeli troops breached the wall and entered the Old City to arrive at the Wailing Wall in 1967.

Armed with Kalashnikovs, Israeli adolescents patrol the dark alleyways. Having passed through the Armenian Quarter, we come to the Arab/Palestinian part of the Old City. A long lane full of leftovers from the day's market bears the marks of explosions. Israeli gangs climb onto the roofs of the market to stone, petrol-bomb and, at times, shoot the Palestinian shoppers.

An iron gate suddenly bars the way; on the other side the walls are clean and white, the street lighting is bright and luminous, the shops do not sell spices or pita bread but jewels, gold, diamonds. The noisy voices of the Arab market fade into the religious and orderly quiet of the Jewish Quarter.

Israel calls itself the state of the Jewish people, not the state of all its citizens. Today there are nearly one million Palestinians living in Israel and they have been discriminated against at all levels since the 'Nakba'. In the early 1990s the late Yitzhak Rabin expressed his 'shame' at the way the state treated its Arab minority. It suffices to recall that two out of three Palestinian children in Israel live below the poverty line.

The dome of a mosque may appear as a shock in a district bearing the Star of David. The Israelis were about to burn it down when Hamas warned that if they even touch it they would cover the Wailing Wall with the settlers' blood. Since then the police have surrounded the Magrabin mosque with a grid and they patrol it 24 hours a day.

Right opposite the First Station of the Cross, a small iron door hides another of the Old City's secrets. It is a tunnel, ordered by the

The entrance to a Jewish Orthodox district in West Jerusalem.

then prime minister Netanyahu and tantamount to the rape of Al-Quds, because the Israelis tunnelled right under the al-Aqsa Mosque and other Muslim sacred sites, to allow the Jews a safe passage to the Wailing Wall. This imposition defies the Oslo Agreement by which Jerusalem should be guaranteed the maintenance of its international status quo. Palestinian opposition to this profanation led to violent clashes with Israeli security forces. Six Palestinians were killed in Jerusalem before the violence spread. In the following three days 62 Palestinians and 15 soldiers were to die.

As Mustapha, born and bred in the Old City, explains:

> Palestinians here, like in the rest of Jerusalem, are tolerated as long as they confine themselves to a ghetto and to a narrow agenda which doesn't include the preservation of their national and cultural identity, and doesn't ensure equality.

The peace process collapsed at Camp David over the fate of Jerusalem, which proved to be one of the thorniest issues in the final status negotiations. A few weeks after the failure of that summit, an Israeli assault on Al-Quds took the form of the provocative visit by Ariel Sharon to the Arab heart of the Old City, marking the start of the second Intifada.

As many Arabs are keen to remind foreigners, each time Israel has tried to curb Palestinian resistance in one place, it has sprung up in another. This happened when the struggle was forced to move from the Territories to Jordan, and later from Jordan to Lebanon, then from Lebanon to the Gaza Strip with the first Intifada, to which Jenin was added during the second one.

Israel has been spared any major Palestinian upheaval in Jerusalem. If that should happen one day, it will make Gaza and Jenin look like sideshows. As leading Israeli newspapers bluntly put it: 'Jerusalem will become a scene of bloodshed for generations unless we have the courage to say, "Yes, it must be divided".'[4]

Before the outbreak of the present Intifada a vast movement (including the city's municipality, pacifist organizations and over 60 percent of the Labour Party) had launched a successful campaign under the slogan 'One City, Capital of Two States'. After Sharon's election, Jerusalem is no longer on the agenda.

The fact is that by conceding double citizenship to the city, the Israeli government would have everything to gain. Israel's recognition of the Palestinians' right to Al-Quds would pave the way for international recognition of its claim to Yerushalayim. And building on this starting point the city might become the engine for peace, an asset rather than a barrier to conflict resolution.

Notes

1. The Israeli parliament.
2 . Gaza and Jericho were returned to the PNA only in 1994, followed by Jenin, Nablus, Ramallah, Bethlehem, Tulkarm and 80 percent of Hebron in 1997.
3. The careful wording used by Israel, 'jurisdiction' or 'administration', has been extended to recently occupied areas. Obviously, international law does not recognize unilateral annexation, even if carried out after 'a war of self-defence', as the Israelis portray the carefully planned invasion in 1967.
4. Source: *Haaretz*, August 30, 2000.

11.

Gaza

It is the largest and most populated open prison in the world – a laager of barbed wire, minefields, watchtowers and trenches, 48 kilometres long and seven wide, wedged in between the Negev desert, the Egyptian border and the Mediterranean.

It is the Kingdom of David for the Israelis, an arid strip of anguish for the Palestinians, strangled by apartheid and asphyxiated in an economic vice which strips them of the right to life and denies them access to food and water, to housing, work and education.

This is the Gaza Strip, a place forgotten by humanity. Its name means exile, homelessness, dispossession, confinement, extermination; it conjures up images of children being murdered, tear gas and barricades.

Paradoxically, there is a deep sense of solitude in the region with the highest population density in the world; over 1,200,000 Palestinians are packed within 65 percent of the territory, while 6,000 Israeli settlers occupy the rest.

Its position on the crossroads between Asia and Africa has ensured it a history as troubled as it is long. Today largely a bastion for Hamas and traditionally a land of strong Islamic values, the Gaza Strip was established by the Israeli-Egyptian peace agreements back in 1949. It was occupied by the IDF during the Six Day War and handed back to Arafat after the Oslo Agreement. It was the cradle of the first Intifada and it is here that the present one reaps the heaviest casualties. About half of the 360 Palestinian children murdered by Israeli forces in the last 19 months have died here.[1]

Because of fear of attacks, the northern gate, at the Erez checkpoint, has only been opened a few times since the 1993 deal. It was here that Kifah, an 18 year-old from the Gaza Strip, died when he was stopped, humiliated, beaten and torn to pieces by the dogs of a settler before being prevented from reaching a hospital. The Israeli side of the checkpoint is a bunker with special fortified passages for people and cars; once past the IDF machine-guns there is a road for the Israelis and the outsiders and a tunnel for the Palestinians. The PNA checkpoint resembles a World War One trench with sandbags and barbed wire – not very useful should heavy tanks advance down the road.

The township around Jabalyia is the first sign of the tragedy. 95,000 refugees live here, the largest and most militant of all the refugee camps in the Strip. In Jenin, which housed 14,000 people, there may be a hundred dead. Who knows what might happen were Operation Defensive Shield extended to the Gaza Strip?

After the Hamas bombing in Rishon Letzion when 16 lives were lost (May 8, 2002), the Israelis massed troops and tanks along the Gaza border but the order to attack was frozen at government level. The IDF faced between 200 and 500 partisans in Jenin and lost at least 23 soldiers. Here they might face an estimated 4-5,000 strong resistance. Israeli sources argued that a sweeping invasion of the Strip would play into the hands of Hamas, which opposes the very existence of a Jewish state and whose militants have had months to prepare lines of defence.

In Jabaliya, where the protest which sparked the first Intifada took place,[2] the desolation and agony are hardly believable. Many houses have collapsed; a carpet of debris is all that remains of those razed to the ground by human madness.

Third-class citizens on their own land, local people travel in carts pulled by stolid donkeys, wading across open sewers in the dusty blaze of the sun. Like arcane laments, the hymns from the mosque's speakers hang in the air above the scrubby sand dunes where children are playing on this Friday, day of prayer. The laughter in their eyes is the same as that of children I met in Colombia, Nicaragua, South Armagh, Bosnia – living in very similar conditions and on the border with death.

Established in the aftermath of the 1948 war, the Gaza camps still house an estimated 700,000 refugees. In some cases the eight camps within the Strip have developed into small-size towns with schools and markets, but conditions remain appalling because of overcrowding, a lack of infrastructure and military repression. Through the so-called peace process Israel has succeeded in ensuring its economic dominion over the Palestinians. When the dust settles on the present Intifada, Israel will emerge economically dominant while the Palestinians will require all kinds of help and remain reliant on Israel, a dependence which led to their misery in the first place.

Says Eyad:

> They kill children to kill the Intifada. And they use different killing methods. We have 80 percent unemployment and those who have a job can't go to work because the checkpoints are closed to them. No work means no food; people get sick; the elderly and small children are dying every day. Deprived of everything, many people have only their lives as a last resort to fight back.

The spire of the mosque protrudes from the white line of roofs; a strong taste of revolution and resistance enshrouds the shattered town. Life is suffering in the slums around Gaza City; large families live in shabby houses, shacks or tents or muddy sand holes, without any food, water or electricity. As a friend from Khan Yunis once told me in a slum flat, 'We were born to suffer. That is our life. We survive to be made submissive and slaughtered.'

People should not be condemned to live in such a manner. Some have erected makeshift tents in the ruins of their destroyed homes, having nowhere else to go; most of these people were refugees already, who escaped from Israeli persecution; now they cannot escape Israeli random bombings. Often their only possessions are a goat to provide milk for the infants and pots used to save and store precious water. The Israeli settlers living in the three Gaza Strip settlements can water their gardens or use as much water as their swimming pools require. At the same time the Israeli army has obstructed with sand more than 200 Palestinian water wells; they have diverted rivers, creeks, canals and nearly all the natural waterways in the Strip.

The Middle East is one of the world's most water-stressed regions and although the issue of water has been negotiated and included in the Oslo Agreement, the Gaza-Jericho Accord of 1995 and the 1995 Interim Agreement, Palestinians have no sovereignty over some of their own natural resources. In the West Bank the Israeli army has seized large areas around rivers which run through Palestinian territory, diverted waterways towards the settlements and denied access to the banks of the River Jordan, which is an international river system.

Beach Camp is home to thousands of children. There are coloured kites in the clouds and crowded carts on the sandy roads. A child has taken his horse to cool down in the Mediterranean. A few yards down the road Gaza City's harbour is ravaged and empty. It contains only two dozen small fishing boats, painted yellow, a small ship sunk by the Israelis while still anchored to the pier, deserted quays.

The white houses flanking the city's roads are pitted with the black bruises of gunshots; in some cases only the facade of the building remains intact and there is nothing behind – Apache and F16 facelifts. They appear like monstrous dolls' houses besieged by children. Israel's anti-terrorism legislation bans Palestinians from building houses with a third floor; however the law, drafted to contain the sniper problem, does not prevent them from building further floors over the forbidden third one. That explains the bizarre architectural trend in the Territories, where many houses are split in two sections of two landings each, separated by pillars and columns.

Children are playing on sand banks placed at the side of the streets. At sunset these mountains will host land mines or other devices, put there as 'safety measures' in case of an Israeli raid. The smell of seaweed signals how close the Mediterranean is. But an archipelago of ruins and rubbish outlines Sharon's path to peace. After the last rounds of bombardment the Strip appears disfigured, gutted.

The presidential palace which made history now lies in ruins. It was here that in December 1998 Arafat convened the Palestinian Council and with American President Clinton as witness, scrapped the destruction of Israel from the Palestinian manifesto.

PNA policemen usually stay in a tent outside the police barracks for fear of air raids. The perimeter wall is intact but what is left of the police station conjures up images of the allied bombing of Dresden in 1944. The remains of a seven-storey building hit by F16 bombs sits by itself, now a bare four or five metres high; each floor has collapsed onto the one beneath it. Police shields and uniforms are trapped between concrete blocks and a jungle of iron structures. Our guides stop before the roof of another building, now just a couple of metres tall, and tell us that we are standing on an unexploded two-ton F16 bomb.

Outside the barracks children jump across sewers as if they were streams of fresh water. Sharon promised to bring peace to the region but it appears quiet obvious that the only peace he intended for his neighbours was the peace of the cemeteries. He portrays Israel as the victim of an unrepentant terrorist aggressor, but seen from the Gaza Strip it is clear who the oppressors are.

This is definitively a place apart. The land is being choked to death by an impenetrable sense of suffocation and plundered by Israel's policy of ethnic cleansing.

From the Shujayya district of the city – where four children, 27 women and 29 men were killed by Israeli mortars commanded by a young officer named Ariel Sharon in April 1956 – as far as the Egyptian border one long expanse of refugee camps stretches out.

Driving along the coastline one can avoid the firing range of Israeli positions but by the seaside the tangible despair that surrounds everything is even more poignant – people living within walls of mud or sand with corrugated iron sheets for roofs and nobody in sight but children.

Behind them there are hundreds of acres of ancient orange groves and slender olive trees; along with strawberries and potatoes they are the only local produce. But as the Israeli government claims these groves provide covers for attackers, they simply uproot those close to the settlements or the army positions; the once-cultivated fields are flattened layers of orange soil, a no-man's land with traces of tank and bulldozer tracks still clearly visible. But oranges, olives, potatoes and strawberries have no politics. Their extirpation has made poor people even poorer and starved more children.

An Israeli battleship scours the horizon's watery wrinkled skin. The Palestinians were given the right to a state, but not to its skies and they have only limited access to the sea; fishing boats must remain within three miles of the coast, where there are no fish. So the fishing boats are lying keel down on the sand, like old cetaceans stranded along deserted beaches.

All the children remain on the side of the road opposite the sea, even though the beach might have provided amusement and recreation. Undercurrents and tides make the water hazardous but obviously that is not the reason. 'Zionist soldiers planted mines and booby traps in many places, often along the coast; five kids were blown to pieces last winter by one such device', recalls a local.

Trawler nets hang to dry in the sunset and barefoot children run along the dusty road peppered with craters which leads to the small settlement of Netzarim.[3] Not even the seagulls dare to land here.

The Palestinian police block the road with sandbags. Israeli infrared sights and 50 mm killing machines are only a few yards away and they shoot anyone that moves. From his position a soldier keeps his eye glued to his telescopic sights, his ear to the mobile phone. One of these troopers, a Sephardic Jew, stationed here in 1991 and known for harassing Arabs, made history. His name was Ygal Amir and four years later he was to murder Yitzhak Rabin.[4]

According to Gazans, despite Amir's links to the ultra-orthodox far-right, the Israelis found a way to make the Palestinians pay for Rabin's untimely death. The Shabak, Israel's internal security service, discovered that one of their own undercover agents had planned the assassination. The fundamentalist Jewish right-wing, which had instigated Rabin's murder, actually won the elections the following year and the Israeli military establishment badly needed to divert attention

A police cap sits in the ruins of a police barracks in Gaza City, after an F16 air-raid.

from the embarrassing episode of the premier's assassination and bring it to focus on the Territories.

Yihye Ayash, one of the leaders of the Islamic armed movement, accused of manufacturing the devices for a devastating bombing campaign, was nicknamed 'the Engineer'. He was in the Gaza Strip when his mobile phone rang. When he answered, it blew up and cut off his head. According to Tel Aviv, during his 'career' he was responsible for the death of 190 Israelis.

Inland, the near-by village of Boureij became the symbol of the Palestinian struggle for survival towards the start of the present Intifada. Jamal al-Duri commuted every day from here to go to work on the outskirts of Tel Aviv. He had seven children. Jamal and his twelve-year old son Mohammed were walking a few yards from an Israeli post near the Netzarim Junction, a well-known flashpoint, when Palestinian gunmen opened fire on the army. Jamal pushed his son into a gap in a wall and hid behind a barrel of cement, while sheltering his son with his own body.

Within minutes the attackers had stopped but the IDF had not. Despite Jamal's screaming and waving the Israelis kept shooting and ten minutes later hit him. He managed to ring for help but a Red Crescent ambulance approaching the scene had to stop because its driver was hit in the head and died immediately. Mohammed was screaming.

The IDF kept shooting at the barrel. The child was clinging to his father's body when a burst of machine-gun fire pierced his tee shirt, striking both him and his father. The bullet which eventually killed Mohammed was fired 20 minutes after the Palestinian gunmen had fled the scene of the attack. Despite having been hit eight times, Jamal, copiously bleeding and crying beside the wall, was still alive.

Hidden by the trees, Deir el-Balah is a large refugee camp partially transformed into a village. In his office outside the camp, Abed holds his grandsons on his knee.

> Children are not afraid to die but they are afraid of the sound of the jet bombers. They don't understand why they bombard us and kill us. We are called terrorists because we

dared to resist. But the state of Israel was born out of terrorism and it was sustained with terrorism. Didn't the Americans defend themselves after the attack on New York and Washington? Of course, we are not all equals. We are the bad ones; we live on the wrong side of the world.

But people should look beyond the prejudices and stereotypes which Israel is disseminating along their murderous way and see what this is all about. It is about state terrorism on the one hand and about freedom on the other. We want to seed this land with hope but they have only death to offer. Sharon's military policy has failed; it didn't produce the surrender of the oppressed but it forced them to pass from throwing stones to blowing up human bombs. That's what he has achieved.

Date palms struggle to block out the last glimpse of dying daylight. A few yards down the road three tank divisions are protecting the settlement of Kfar Darom, home to only 40 Jewish Orthodox families.

There is no way to reach Khan Yunnis and Rafiah because a convoy of settlers is driving out of the Strip; it is too far and too risky to head north towards Erez, the Egyptian frontier prevents them from going south and they can only move eastward. When they do so, the Strip is literally slit into three sections and the Israeli army will not let anyone across. Borders within borders, open prisons within open prisons – the Gaza Strip is where human dignity ends.

'We have a few weapons and less ammunition but we can still face and fight the Israeli army. But when they come from the sky there is nothing we can do; there's no place to hide', says a young Palestinian while children pose beside a mural.

I cannot help imagining how their parents reacted when they received the bodies of their three sons. The boys had just watched the horrors of Jenin on the news and decided to do something about it; they told everyone they were going out for a walk. Armed with knives, they crawled under the barbed wire surrounding an Israeli settlement but they were spotted by the

IDF and killed with machine-gun fire. After the shooting a bulldozer drove over the children's bodies which were then thrown to the army dogs before being returned to their families.

Mute lamp poles, blackened windows, flickering bonfires – Gaza's nights are peopled with darkness and darkness is alive with fear. Wisps of fog advance from the Mediterranean. The deep awesome silence is broken only by dogs howling and children crying. Even the distant thunder of a passenger plane makes eyes search for signs of death in the sky. All around stand the walls of the laager, and there is nowhere to go, nowhere to be.

Notes

1. That is the official figure for children under the age of 14. According to the PNA Ministry for Health the actual number is 467 (that includes all children under 18). The report states that 450 Israelis and an estimated 2,280 Palestinians have lost their lives since September 2000. The number of registered Palestinians killed in the Gaza Strip is 626 (9,312 wounded) while 977 have died in the West Bank (18,688 injured). In addition 663 people died as a direct result of checkpoint closure and economic apartheid.

2. In December 1987, an Israeli lorry driver killed four young Palestinians. It was the spark that ignited the first uprising. During the funerals people invoked the 'Jihad', the Holy War. The word 'Intifada', used for the Palestinian revolt, was adopted for the first time by Hamas. And although it was not Hamas (established in Gaza in the late 1980s) but the atrocious conditions imposed by the Israelis that started the Intifada, just like the Soweto uprising ten years earlier, the group (Hamas is the anachronism of Harakat al-Mukawma al-Islamiya, the Islamic Resistance Movement), played a fundamental role in it.

3. Too isolated and exposed to possible Palestinian incursion. For years now, military advisers have been urging the Tel Aviv authorities to dismantle the small colony.

4. Rabin openly said, 'I wish the Gaza Strip would sink into the sea', so great were its problems, so unruly its people.

12.

Searching

First they came for the Communists,
and I didn't speak up,
because I wasn't a Communist.
Then they came for the Jews,
and I didn't speak up,
because I wasn't a Jew.
Then they came for the Catholics,
and I didn't speak up,
because I was a Protestant.
Then they came for me,
and by that time there was no one
left to speak up for me.

Father Martin Niemoller's words are inscribed on the shady wall among the relics and the pale photographs, lit only by a candle. Erected on the top of one of Jerusalem's hills, Yad Vashem is the Holocaust Museum, where six millions Jews exterminated by the Nazis before 1945 are commemorated. Inside the building is like reliving the horror. Tins of Zyklon B poison pellets used to gas women and children, their dolls turned ghostly by barbarity and aging. Outside in the gardens, screaming skulls and hands stretched out are chained into scary iron sculptures in blocks of six: six candlesticks, six Stars of David, etc., one for each million Jews.

My family has a solid tradition of partisan resistance against the Germans and I was bred with its memories. I have seen concentration camps in San Saba, in the far north-east of Italy, and Dachau, just outside the Bavarian city of Munich. But if the Yad Vashem corridors are just as breathtaking as the crematorium chambers, leaving the museum, I felt confused, wondering if I am guilty of offending the memory of six million dead. Yet having seen the appalling conditions in Jenin, Aida or Gaza City, it is hard to imagine how a people who suffered such an evil can be capable of inflicting the same ordeal on anyone else. In no way is this an attempt to make any comparison between the Holocaust and the Israel-Palestine question; furthermore, in my entire life I have upheld and defended a philosophy of anti-nazism and anti-Semitism. It is just that, of all people on this planet, no one is better placed than the Jews to realize that the racism which characterizes the present Israeli leadership can only lead to ethnic cleansing.[1] They belong to the most persecuted people, which should make them the greatest enemies of racism.

And many who then condemned the Nazis are now taking part in the new genocide against the Palestinians – some by providing means of mass destruction, some simply by remaining silent, blind to facts. What does the world expect from a people, occupied and oppressed, having already ceded 78 percent of their land?

According to UN Resolution number 181, the birth of a Palestinian state should have come about at the same time as Israel; in fact, Israel's legitimacy is bound to the full implementation of the resolution. Yet the inalienable right of the Palestinians to their state has not been defended.

Humiliated every day in the eyes of the world and strangled by a form of economic apartheid which is quietly killing possibly more people, the elderly and children in particular, than the IDF itself, Palestinians are dying amid the total indifference and the tacit compliancy of all. The very international community which, back in 1982, pledged to defend their camps outside Beirut after the PLO left, is abandoning the Palestinian people again – exactly as it did 20 years ago and at the mercy of the same warlords.

The implicit premise is that Israel needs protection from the Palestinians and not vice versa. And here lies the rub. Not only is Israel forgiven for its 35 years of occupation, for its 54 years of exploitation of the entire Palestinian people and its oppression characterised by an unbelievable series of barbarities of which Jenin is simply the latest example, but it is rewarded with the annexation of the best land available on the West Bank, the cancellation of the refugees' right to return, with the legal right to design the Palestinian borders (Palestine cannot border on any other country than Israel).

From what I have witnessed here, this is not a war; 'war' suggests a parity in strength and violence. This is a military occupation. On the one side there is the most powerful army in the region; on the other one there is only a civilian population. This is a 54 year-old conflict without a front line, without historical, geographical or moral borders.

After Jenin and Operation Defensive Shield nothing will be the same again – and not because of the deportations, nor because of the suffering and the mourning which will breed more mourning. The Israelis will not retreat; they will not get back within their borders; they will expand them with the new buffer zone which will transform Palestine into a maze of bantustans, caging millions of people into open prisons.

Far from bringing security, the 10 kilometre deep and 360 kilometre long exclusion zone (the wall of electric barbed-wire and cement will cost $1 million per kilometre) means annexing 58 percent of the occupied Territories. The Palestinians living in villages within these zones will have to be deported, their towns razed to the ground, just like in 1948. The difference now is that the Palestinians no longer flee.

Dr. Ashrawi's words echoed in my ears.

> What Sharon really wants is…a full-scale reoccupation of the West Bank and the Gaza Strip, in his own terms a legal extension of the military occupation. Needless to say it would lead to a new wave of violence and it would generate more resistance. It is simply a justification to legitimise the submission of our people.

For the Palestinians it is still difficult to comprehend why they must be treated in such an atrocious way. Was it really necessary to inflict a collective punishment on three and a half million people only to kill or arrest a few hundred partisans?

The blood from its wounds flowing through Jenin's alleyways may have ceased but it should not be allowed to go unnoticed. Victims of human rights abuses, in Jenin and on the West Bank, are entitled to justice. And maybe they have reasons to ask why the international community has not responded the way it did in other circumstances.

On April 19, the UN Security Council voted unanimously to dispatch a 'fact finding mission' to Jenin. Israeli Foreign Minister Shimon Peres welcomed the investigation, 'which will help to clarify the facts on what happened in Jenin. We have nothing to hide. Our hands are clean'.[2] But while publicly welcoming the mission, Israel was doing everything possible to stop it.

The US administration came to Sharon's rescue by threatening to use their veto and the decision to defy international opinion was taken after assurances from Washington that it would not pressure Sharon over Jenin in return for lifting the siege against Yasser Arafat[3] – 'free Ramallah to free Jenin', as the Tel Aviv media emphasized.

Obviously providing Israel with further impunity (they have already ignored nearly 80 UN resolutions) will only encourage instability and war.

Because of the Israeli refusal the UN investigation team was disbanded in early June 2002. Since there was no proper investigation, the true story of Jenin remains largely untold and Israel's official version that nothing even remotely resembling a massacre took place, became accepted. More frightening still, it enabled Israel to recover its most precious title: that of victims.

Can the Israeli refusal not be read as an admission of guilt?

'An Arab poet once wrote: "My house? Here it is; a drop of dew between the petals of a rose",' quotes an old lady sitting on the floor of her shattered home. She has not heard from her husband since he was deported back in April.

Exactly three months after the IDF attack was launched I came back to Jenin on a sunny morning. When I entered the refugee camp during the Israeli attack, the smoke of the fires, the dust of the debris and the tanks prevented me from seeing the sky. But now the sky is so bright and clear and it looks infinitely deep. I feel as if I were returning.

The city, with its refugee camp, is intact. As the Israelis still refuse to allow any equipment in, the ruins are still where they stood. The horror remains undiminished.

Only the people have changed. Like in the rest of the West Bank, after the official end of Operation Defensive Shield, the IDF withdrew only from a few pockets of human misery that continue to be encircled by military units and settlers. In the case of Jenin, Israeli artillery and Merkavas can be seen on the hill facing the city. Three months ago the camp was almost deserted; now it is teeming with children and old people – sunken faces, sorrowful eyes, deeply wounded souls, half-naked kids, skin and bone, their eyes wide with hunger; they wander among the mine fields and the derelict houses. There is almost no sign of the adult male population.

There are corpses still rotting in 'Jeningrad' and people whose fate is still unknown; according to the locals those missing number 1,200. Of these 700 are still detained in Israeli prisons. One hundred and fifty bodies have already been identified but there is still no official confirmation of the fate of the missing partisans.[4]

Hanat al Hawashin, the district in the centre of the camp is still an unbelievable sight. Like ash from a mass grave, the windblown dust from the ruins comes to rest on the entire city, greying its colours, choking its perfumes, aging its hearts. The people have made a path through 'ground zero' to take a short cut along the hill. Some old men pause to look at the mayhem. Shreds of dolls and bits of toys are still to be found amid the tangled mess of wire and debris. Locals grunt that many dead bodies have never been recovered and no one knows exactly how many there are.

Many people are living in the ruins of their homes. Some are staying with relatives in Jenin. Many locals return every day trying to save something from the rubble of their houses; some are still searching for survivors. They have lost everything; most of them do not even own a pair of shoes, courtesy of IDF's 'humanity'. Humanitarian aid, food and medicine barely manage to trickle through because of the military siege. Water and electricity have returned only to a few small pockets within the camp, while the military repression goes on unabated. Since April the massacre has not stopped; war crimes, illegal killings and human rights abuses continue on a daily basis in Jenin. A few days ago two children asked their father's permission to go to buy a bar of chocolate. As there were no IDF troops in sight and the grocer's shop was around the corner, Jamil (11) and Ahmen (6) took their bicycle to get there. They were returning home when a Merkava surprised them from behind, killing the two boys with two shells at close range. Ahmed was buried with the chocolate bar clutched in his hands.

The IDF has recently made a series of quieter invasions into the city and locals have every reason to expect new and bigger raids. They claim the Israelis do not want to remove the rubble from the camp because the ruins will make it more accessible next time the Merkavas thunder in. As a direct consequence, even the donations for the people in the camp from western organizations have petered out; what is the point in investing in reconstruction when the IDF is waiting to destroy it?

The old premier claims assaults and executions 'are necessary to reopen the peace negotiations and establish peace and security' but his goal is the complete reoccupation of the Territories and, as seen in Jenin, he is prepared to perpetrate evil crimes to achieve this. It does not matter how many Palestinians and Israelis will have to be sacrificed.

Some observers suggest that after the latest attack on the West Bank and with the option of exiling Arafat still open, the Israeli premier may opt for a transitional solution: allowing a Palestinian state only in the Gaza Strip. This means courting utter disaster, the results of which are unpredictable.

Maybe the prophecy of those Israelis who, back in 1967, warned that triumph might gradually turn into defeat and compromise Israel's democratic identity, are being proved right. As for myself and those who believe in the self-determination of two peoples, mutually and equally, there can be no military solution. The IDF should pull out of the Territories; it would only take around two months to withdraw soldiers and settlers from 90 percent of the West Bank.

But it is the Palestinians who seem most in need of security, of protection from a vengeful and heinous form of state terrorism. It is not Israel which is in danger; it is the Palestinians who are being systematically killed on a daily basis.

The journey's diary has no epilogue as, at the moment of concluding my account (in Gaza, in July 2002), Israel's criminal policy remains virtually unaltered and unchallenged – although somewhat prudently, some of the Arab states are beginning to surge with nationalist sentiments to the point of using the oil threat. In preparation for the worst, Syria has moved its tank divisions closer to the Lebanon and the Golan Heights; the Hizbullah are still launching mortar attacks on the north of Israel and mass demonstrations in Jordan and Egypt have helped to create a very volatile environment.

It is not just Palestine but the whole of the Middle East that is being threatened by the IDF tanks. Israel is the only country in the region to own nuclear weapons, about four hundred of them. They can be armed on the 237 F16s supplied by the Americans[5] and are also installed on three submarines, a gift from Germany, which now patrol the Red Sea, the Mediterranean and the Persian Gulf. This means that there is a gun loaded with nuclear weapons aimed at the temple of the Arab states.

Shamefully, the turmoil of conflict is met only by the world's silence. The UN has produced almost 80 Resolutions, the first one in 1948, but it has done nothing to implement them. The European countries should stop asking the US to find a solution to a problem for which they bear the responsibility. Europe made

life a misery for millions of Jews and made their demand for a
state legitimate in the aftermath of the Holocaust, in which the
Palestinians had no hand.

More than anyone else, the European Union should pressurize
the United States into supporting the deployment of international
observers since the Palestinians are still paying for our anti-
semitic racism. This seems the only viable prelude to urgent
peace talks designed to draw Israel's illegitimate occupation to a
conclusion. Sharon insists that Arafat should stop terrorism
before he recalls his armed forces. But Israeli withdrawal is an
internationally recognized right of the Palestinian people; it
should not be regarded as a concession.

In light of such injustice, even President Bush, Sharon's
strongest protector, asks Tel Aviv to pull out of the Territories
because he needs to secure a reduction of violence in Palestine.
In the short term, the Americans had to take the Arab League[6] on
board to guarantee the next step in their global witch-hunt, Iraq.
In the long term, within the 'new global order', they cannot rely
on only two allies (Turkey and Israel) in the region to counter
the latest threats from the 'new enemy' based in some nearby
Islamic states. That is why, despite so much violence, a ceasefire
in Palestine, on American's conditions, may still be achieved;
sadly, it will not defuse the time bomb, only postpone the
explosion.

At the end of the spring in Jenin, when a convoy loaded with
boxes full of tents, food and toys from the United States Agency
for International Development (USAID) arrived in the camp,
people refused to open the parcels and sent the convoy back
along the road it came from. 'Our houses have been destroyed by
missiles and tanks and our people have been murdered with
American military hardware in the hands of Israeli soldiers', they
explained. 'We would prefer to die from starvation rather than be
fed by our assassins'.

'The future is dying', says Bush and for once no one can say he
is wrong, 'It will be a transitory one, with no power or sovereignty

but we are committing ourselves to make a Palestinian state a reality'. On Mars, maybe. And without the Palestinians. There will hardly be anyone left if Sharon is not stopped.

Under Sharon equality is impossible. The only peace possible is that whose terms are dictated by Israel and the United States. Occupation and oppression are destined to stay. This should be no reason to accept the injustice.

Notes

1. Even some of those who survived Dachau and other death factories, for the very first time, last winter went as far as to accuse their premier of 'insulting those who died in the Holocaust with his policy of mass executions'. Accusing the Palestinians, and those who support them, of being anti-semitic, has been a long-standing tactic used by successive Israeli governments; Prime Minister Begin said there was no difference between Arafat and Hitler while his successor in the Knesset, Yitzhak Shamir, declared that the Palestinian wish for an independent state is tantamount to a second 'final solution'.
2. *Ha' Aretz*, 23/4/2002.
3. On May 1, after a five month siege, the Palestinian President was declared 'free to move within the Territories', in exchange for the handover (to an American-British body) of those accused of the murder of Israel's racist minister Revaham Zeevi, killed in October 2001 by the Popular Front for the Liberation of Palestine (PFLP), along with the man who allegedly masterminded the intercepted shipment of illegal weapons, in January. Founded in 1967 by George Habash, the once Marxist-Leninist group with an uncompromising stance towards Israel stepped up its campaign in the present Intifada. In August 2001 the IDF killed its leader, Ali Abu Mustapha, with a rocket fired into his office in retaliation for Zeevi's killing.
4. Amnesty International's report later confirmed these accusations. It reviewed the death of 54 Palestinians who died between April 3 and 17 in Jenin, all of whose names were on hospital lists. The figure includes seven women, four children and six men over the age of 55. However, not included are the Palestinians who were not registered as refugees with UNRWA, some of the fighters, those from surrounding villages and the bodies which have never been found (spirited away, buried on the spot, crushed by tanks and bulldozers).
5. 102 American F16s (each worth $34 million) are on the way to Israel. In addition the United States has already sold Tel Aviv 50

F4E Phantoms ($18.5 million each) and 98 F15 Eagles, both made by Boeing, second supplier to the Pentagon. This means that the US has supplied Israel with 487 modern, dual capacity planes. Israel also has the most sophisticated military helicopters in the world: 57 Cobra Attack, 42 AH-64 Apache Attack, 38 Sea Stallion and 25 Blackhawks, with a cost varying between $11 and $15 million each. All this contradicts American law on arms exports which bans their use for non-defensive purposes. The powerful Israeli war machine costs $9 billion a year, equal to 20 percent of the national budget. Half of this cost is footed by the US which in return receives most of it back as arms payments.

6. The 22 Arab countries, including Libya and Iran, would effectively recognize Israel and its right to exist in the context of the Saudi peace offer launched in March: a return to the pre-1967 borders in exchange for security.

Hoping to return one day. Palestinian refugees took the keys of their houses with them when they were exiled. The photograph was taken in Bethlehem.

Postscript

The manuscript was at an editorial stage when, at the end of July 2002, the long-awaited UN report on the Jenin events was finally published.

Kofi Annan states that the report was compiled without a visit to Jenin by UN officers. Also, the United Nations had requested full co-operation from both sides of the community but only received it partially from the Palestinian Authority. Except from T. Larsen and a few volunteers, no one from the UN body visited Jenin.

The UN Secretary General underlines that the report is based mainly on eye witness reports by international observers, UNRWA personnel and Red Cross personnel, even if all of them were banned from entering Jenin until the end of the operation. 'These were the only accessible sources of information for this report.'

The report outlines how 'Operation Defensive Shield was characterized by extensive curfews on civilian populations and restrictions, indeed occasional prohibitions, on the movement of international personnel, including at times humanitarian and medical personnel as well as human rights monitors and journalists'.

Highlighting that 'Israel's obligations in the Occupied Palestinian Territory are set out in the Geneva Convention relative to the Protection of Civilian Persons in Time of War, to which Israel is a High Contracting Party', the UN seems to confirm the worst case scenario.

However, according to Kofi Annan the responsibility should be equally shared by both parties.

Combatants on both sides conducted themselves in ways that, at times, placed civilians in harm's way. Much of the fighting during Operation Defensive Shield occurred in areas heavily populated by civilians, in large because the armed Palestinian groups sought by the IDF placed their combatants and installation among civilians.

But in Jenin, as in Nablus or the Church of the Nativity, there was simply nowhere else to go.

The number of 500 dead given by the Palestinian Authority as a final count is, according to Annan, an approximate estimate of all Palestinians who died between March and early May 2002 in the West Bank. According to the report, 'at least 52 Palestinians, of whom up to a half may have been civilians, and 23 Israeli soldiers were dead' in Jenin. Even Kofi Annan has to admit that these numbers cannot be regarded as definite: 'It is impossible to determine with precision how many civilians were among the Palestinian dead'.

'In April 2002, some 200 armed men from the al-Aqsa Martyrs Brigades, Palestinian Islamic Jihad and Hamas, operated from the Jenin camp', but the UN cannot come up with evidence to demonstrate that Israel eliminated those 200 men. They simply vanished and the report fails to explain their fate.

Approximately 150 buildings had been destroyed and many others were rendered structurally unsound. There are reports that between the 5th and the 9th of April, the IDF increased missile strikes from the helicopters and the use of bulldozers – including their use to demolish homes and allegedly bury beneath them those who refused to surrender – and engaged in indiscriminate firing.

Notwithstanding its superficiality, the UN report outlines how Israel is responsible for committing war crimes such as executions, torture, using civilians as human shields, while the Palestinians are blamed for 'basing themselves in a densely populated civilian area and the use of children to transport and possibly lay booby-traps'. It is furthermore confirmed that the

IDF was responsible for mistreating medical personnel. Doctors were killed, ambulances shot at, preventing the injured from reaching the hospital and therefore bleeding to death.

The question is no longer whether Israel is guilty of war crimes and crimes against humanity. The core question is how to prevent Israel from 'creating' other Jenins.